Life & Health

Insurance

TEST PREP

Ace Your License at First Try!

Q&A | Tests | Extra Study Aids

Bennett Lane

Unlock Your Study Aids Now – Download Available!

- **INCLUDES AUDIOBOOK** for on-the-go learning.

- **DIGITAL COPY OF THIS BOOK** to have with you at all times for revision whenever and wherever you want.

- **XL PACK**: access the **"*Property & Casualty Insurance Test Prep*" in digital format** at no additional cost.

- **"GUIDE TO INSURANCE TERMS" flashcards (over 1000!)** in PDF format ready to print and in .APKG format for Anki app, for a dynamic and interactive learning experience.

- **Direct contact** for assistance or clarifications, ensuring continuous support in your preparation.

TABLE OF CONTENTS

INTRODUCTION

Welcome to the world of life and health insurance! Whether you're a fresh face eager to dive into the intricacies of the industry or a seasoned professional seeking to sharpen your skills for the licensing exam, this guide is your compass. Embarking on this journey might seem daunting at first, but rest assured, you've made a commendable choice. The path to understanding and mastering the concepts of life and health insurance is not just about passing an exam; it's about laying the foundation for a rewarding career that makes a difference in people's lives.

The insurance sector, with its rich history and ever-evolving nature, is a fascinating realm. It's an industry built on the principles of trust, care, and foresight—qualities that resonate deeply in the services provided to individuals and communities. As you step into this world, you're not just learning policies and regulations; you're becoming a part of a community that safeguards people's futures and well-being.

This book is designed to be your steadfast companion through the complexities of life and health insurance exam prep. We'll start with a bird's-eye view of the insurance sector, laying out the fundamental principles that govern it. You'll gain insights into the types of life and health policies, understanding not just their structure but the spirit behind their provisions, riders, options, and exclusions.

As we delve deeper, we'll explore the nuances of policy underwriting and issuance, unravel the considerations for retirement and taxation, and shed light on effective management strategies. This journey will also take us through the latest trends and challenges in the insurance industry, preparing you to navigate the future landscape with confidence and expertise.

Join us as we embark on this enlightening journey, equipped with the knowledge and skills to thrive in the insurance sector. Your future in shaping secure and resilient communities starts here.

At its core, the insurance industry represents a promise—a pledge to protect individuals, families, and businesses from the unforeseen and the inevitable. It's a sector defined by its commitment to upholding financial security and peace of mind in the face of uncertainties. Insurance's magic lies in its ability to transform risk into reassurance, offering a safety net that spans various aspects of life and health.

The journey of insurance is as old as civilization itself, originating from the basic human instinct to protect one's community. Ancient traders minimized their losses by distributing cargo across multiple vessels, a principle that echoes in today's complex insurance models. From these humble beginnings, insurance has evolved into a sophisticated network of services, regulations, and products designed to meet the diverse needs of modern society.

Insurance operates on several fundamental principles, including risk pooling, the law of large numbers, and the transfer of risk. These concepts work in harmony to create a stable and predictable framework for managing financial risk. By pooling resources and spreading risk among many, insurance providers can offer protection against significant losses, ensuring that no one bears the brunt of misfortune alone.

Within the vast expanse of the insurance industry, life and health insurance stand out for their direct impact on individuals' well-being and financial stability. Life insurance offers a beacon of security for families facing the loss of a loved one, while health insurance provides a critical safety net in managing healthcare costs. These sectors navigate the delicate balance between offering comprehensive coverage and maintaining affordability, a challenge that requires constant innovation and adaptation.

The insurance industry is at a crossroads, with technological advancements and changing consumer expectations driving a wave of innovation. From telematics and wearable devices to artificial intelligence and big data analytics, new tools and technologies are reshaping how risks are assessed and policies are designed. These developments promise to make insurance more personalized, accessible, and efficient, heralding a new era of protection and peace of mind.

As we delve into the intricacies of life and health insurance, remember that you are stepping into a field characterized by its profound impact on individuals' lives and society's welfare. With every policy written and every claim processed, the insurance industry fulfills its promise to serve as a guardian against uncertainty, embodying the timeless human values of care, support, and mutual protection.

The licensing exam for life and health insurance agents is more than a mere hurdle to professional entry; it represents a critical juncture in the journey of aspiring insurance professionals. This examination tests not only one's knowledge of policy structures, legal regulations, and ethical practices but also the ability to apply this knowledge in practical, real-world scenarios. The successful navigation of this exam paves the way for a career filled with opportunities to make meaningful impacts on individuals' lives and financial security.

The Purpose and Importance of the Licensing Exam: The licensing exam serves a dual purpose: ensuring that candidates possess a foundational understanding of insurance principles and are prepared to uphold the industry's standards of practice. This safeguard protects the public from misinformation and unethical practices and ensures that licensed professionals can offer competent and reliable guidance.

Structure of the Exam

Core Components: The exam is structured to cover the breadth of life and health insurance knowledge, including policy types, underwriting processes, insurance law, and ethics. This section will delve into the specific topics covered, the format of questions, and the scoring system, providing candidates with a clear understanding of what to expect.

Test Format and Duration: Understanding the format—multiple-choice, scenario-based questions, etc.—and the allocated time is crucial for effective preparation and time management during the exam. This section offers strategies for approaching different question types and managing exam time efficiently.

Study Strategies and Resources

Recommended Study Materials: This includes a review of endorsed textbooks, online resources, and practice exams that have proven invaluable for candidates preparing for the exam. It also includes a discussion on how to select resources that match one's learning style and study habits.

Study Plans and Schedules: Here are tips on creating an effective study plan, including how to break down the material into manageable sections, schedule study sessions, and balance preparation with other commitments.

Common Challenges and How to Overcome Them

Navigating Difficult Topics: Insight into the topics that candidates typically find challenging and strategies for mastering these areas. This includes practical advice on seeking help, using supplementary resources, and applying knowledge in practical contexts.

Test Anxiety and Stress Management: Strategies for managing test anxiety, staying focused, and maintaining confidence throughout the study process and on exam day. This part emphasizes the importance of mental and physical well-being in exam success.

After the Exam

Interpreting Results: Guidance on what to do after receiving exam results, including how to interpret scores and understand the implications of licensing.

Retake Policies and Strategies: For those who fail to pass on the first attempt, this section provides information on retake policies, waiting periods, and strategies for revising and reapproaching the exam with confidence.

The successful completion of the licensing exam marks the beginning of a promising career in the life and health insurance industry. This final part reflects on the journey ahead, emphasizing continued learning, professional development, and the impact that dedicated insurance professionals can have on their clients and the broader community.

LIFE POLICIES

Navigating the realm of life insurance policies requires a keen understanding of their intricacies and the protections they offer. Life insurance, at its essence, is a contract between an individual and an insurer designed to provide financial security to beneficiaries upon the policyholder's passing. However, the variety and complexity of life insurance policies available today necessitate a more profound exploration to truly grasp their benefits, limitations, and suitability for different life stages and needs.

Types of Life Insurance Policies

Term Life Insurance: This section will dissect term life insurance, a cost-effective and straightforward option that covers the policyholder for a specific period. We will delve into how premiums are determined, the significance of the term length, and the conditions under which the policy pays out.

Whole Life Insurance: complete life insurance offers protection for the complete policyholder's lifetime. It promises a death benefit in addition to a monetary value component. We'll explore the mechanics of cash value, how these policies differ from term life insurance, and the factors influencing their higher premiums.

Universal Life Insurance: Universal life insurance products prioritize flexibility by enabling policyholders to modify their death benefits and premiums over time. This section will cover the investment element of these policies, the impact of interest rates, and the policy's cash value considerations.

Variable Life and Variable Universal Life Insurance: These plans let policyholders invest the policy's cash worth in other accounts in addition to providing death protection. We'll examine the risks and rewards associated with the policy's investment options and how they affect the policy's overall value.

Key Features of Life Policies

Premiums: An exploration of how premiums are calculated across different types of life insurance, including factors like age, health, policy type, and coverage amount.

Death Benefit: This part will detail the death benefit's role in life insurance, including how it is determined, options for payout, and tax implications.

Cash Value: For policies with a savings component, we'll dissect the concept of cash value, including how it accumulates, ways to access it, and its implications for the policy's death benefit and premiums.

Riders and Additions

Accelerated Death Benefit Rider: Additional riders that policyholders may add to their policies to access death benefit funds in certain situations, such terminal sickness, are explained.

Waiver of Premium Rider: Here we'll take a look at how this rider works to cover premiums in the event that the policyholder is unable to work due to a disability.

Guaranteed Insurability Rider: Details on riders that allow the policyholder to purchase additional coverage without further proof of insurability.

Choosing the Right Policy

Assessing Your Needs: Guidance on evaluating personal and financial situations to determine the suitable type of life insurance.

Comparing Policies: Advice on what to look for when comparing different policies, including premiums, benefits, riders, and company reputation.

Consulting with a Professional
The value of talking to an insurance agent or financial planner before purchasing life insurance.
The chapter will wrap up with a reflection on the importance of understanding life insurance policies in depth. It will stress the importance of policyholders and their families making educated decisions since a good life insurance policy may provide financial stability and peace of mind.

Term Life Insurance: An Essential Guide

Term life insurance stands as a pillar of financial planning for those seeking straightforward, affordable coverage. Unlike its permanent counterparts, the purpose of term life insurance is to provide financial security for a certain amount of time, making it an ideal choice for individuals at various stages of life. The basics of term life insurance will be covered in this section, offering a comprehensive understanding of its structure, benefits, and strategic use in financial planning.

The Basics of Term Life Insurance

Defining Term Life Insurance: Term life insurance only provides temporary financial stability for a specified number of years, usually between five and thirty. Term life insurance is the type of policy that possesses insurance benefits for a certain year period with the same low fixed premium value set.

How Term Life Insurance Works: An examination of the mechanics behind term life insurance, focusing on premium calculations, coverage periods, and the process of filing a claim. This segment aims to demystify the operational aspects, making it easier for individuals to understand how term life insurance functions as a safety net for beneficiaries.

Advantages of Term Life Insurance

Affordability: The price of term life insurance in comparison to permanent life insurance choices is one of its most alluring aspects. This section will discuss how the lack of a cash value component and the temporary nature of coverage contribute to lower premiums.

Simplicity: The straightforwardness of term life insurance is a significant advantage for policyholders. This part will highlight the ease of choosing a policy, with fixed premiums and a precise coverage period, making term life insurance an accessible option for many.

Flexibility: Despite its simplicity, term life insurance provides flexibility with regard to the duration of coverage and, in some situations, the ability to convert to a permanent policy. Policyholders have a number of options, such as the ability to renew or convert their policies, which will be discussed in this section.

Selecting the Right Term Life Insurance Policy

Assessing Your Coverage Needs: A manual for assessing financial and personal circumstances to choose the right level of coverage and duration. This part will offer advice on considering debts, income replacement, and future financial obligations when selecting a term life insurance policy.

Comparing Term Life Insurance Policies: Tips on what to look for when comparing different term life insurance policies, including premium costs, company reliability, and the terms of policy conversion. This section will emphasize the importance of thorough research and comparison shopping to find the best policy.

The Role of a Financial Advisor: The decision to purchase term life insurance should be informed by professional advice. In this section, we'll go over the ways in which working with a financial adviser might provide tailored advice, ensuring that the chosen policy aligns with broader economic goals.

Term Life Insurance Considerations and Pitfalls

The Temporary Nature of Coverage: An examination of the implications of term life insurance's temporary coverage, including what happens when a policy expires and the potential need for ongoing insurance as one ages.

Policy Renewal and Premium Increases
This section will address the potential for premium increases upon policy renewal, highlighting the financial considerations of maintaining coverage beyond the initial term.

Conversion Options and Limitations: For those considering converting their term policy to a permanent one, this part will detail the conversion process, associated costs, and timing considerations to ensure policyholders make informed decisions.

Is Term Life Insurance Right for You?

The final section will reflect on the role of term life insurance in a comprehensive financial plan, considering its benefits and limitations. It will encourage readers to weigh their options carefully, considering their current needs, future goals, and the potential for changes in their financial situation.

Whole Life Insurance

Also known as permanent life insurance, whole life insurance provides both a death payment and an increasing cash value over time, ensuring future financial stability. The insured individual may be certain that this insurance coverage will continue to cover them for as long as they live. It provides a combination of protection and savings that may be very important for long-term financial planning.

Understanding Whole Life Insurance

The Core Features
- **Guaranteed Death Benefit:** Ensures beneficiaries receive a predetermined amount upon the policyholder's death, offering financial stability and peace of mind.
- **Fixed Premiums:** Premiums are set at the policy's inception and do not increase with age or changing health conditions, making long-term budgeting simpler.
- Cash Value Accumulation: A fraction of each premium payment adds to a cash value that increases gradually, providing a tangible benefit that the policyholder may borrow against or remove under certain circumstances.

The Benefits of Whole Life Insurance
- **Lifetime Coverage:** Protect yourself for the rest of your life with whole life insurance, ensuring that your financial responsibilities are covered no matter when you pass away.
- **Financial Growth:** A whole life policy's assured growth in cash value offers an extra source of funds for unforeseen expenses or opportunities.
- **Estate Planning:** Estate planning is one possible application for the death benefit, helping to cover estate taxes and providing a legacy for heirs.

Comparing Whole Life to Other Life Insurance Products

- **Term vs. Whole Life:** Whole life insurance provides permanent coverage together with supplementary savings advantages, in contrast to term life insurance which only protects you for a specified time.
- **Universal Life Insurance:** Whole life insurance provides more reliable and consistent prices and benefits in contrast to the variable premiums and death benefits of universal life insurance.

The Cash Value Component Explained

How It Works
- The cash value of a whole-life policy accumulates without being taxed at a predetermined rate established by the insurance provider. This growth is supported by the insurer's general account performance and the policy's premium payments.

Accessing Cash Value
- **Loans:** Policyholders have access to low-interest loans secured by the cash value. However, outstanding loans will reduce the death benefit if not repaid.
- **Withdrawals:** Partial withdrawals may be possible, but they can reduce both the cash value and death benefit.

Strategic Uses
- **Retirement Income:** The cash value can supplement retirement savings, providing a tax-advantaged income stream.
- **Emergency Fund:** It may function as a financial contingency plan for unforeseen expenditures.

Premiums and Cost Considerations

- **Initial Costs:** The cash value and everlasting coverage of whole life insurance make it more costly than term insurance.
- **Long-Term Value:** The fixed premiums and growing cash value can offer long-term financial benefits, making it a valuable part of a comprehensive financial plan.

Choosing the Right Whole Life Policy

- **Assessing Insurer Stability and Reputation:** Choosing a financially stable company is crucial for long-term policies like whole life insurance.
- **Policy Features and Riders:** Understanding available riders and policy features can help tailor the coverage to your specific needs.

Common Misconceptions

- **Too Expensive:** While premiums are higher, the long-term value and living benefits can outweigh the costs for many individuals.
- **Unnecessary if You Have Term Insurance:** Whole life offers benefits beyond death protection, including cash value growth and estate planning advantages.

Is Whole Life Insurance Right for You?

Choosing whole life insurance involves considering your financial goals, the need for lifelong coverage, and the value of a growing cash value. For those seeking a stable, long-term insurance solution that contributes to their financial security and planning, whole life insurance can be a cornerstone of a well-rounded financial strategy.

Flexible Protection for a Changing World

In the diverse world of life insurance, Universal Life (UL) Insurance stands out for its flexibility and adaptability to the policyholder's changing financial circumstances. Unlike its more rigid counterparts, The stability of permanent life insurance is combined with the adaptability of flexible rates and benefits in universal life insurance. This makes it an attractive option for those who seek lifelong coverage but also want the ability to adjust their financial planning as their life evolves.

Core Features of Universal Life Insurance

Adjustable Premiums: The flexibility to modify premium payments within certain bounds is a signature feature of universal life insurance. This section will explain how policyholders can increase or decrease their premium costs based on their current financial situation and how these adjustments affect the policy's cash value and death benefit.

Flexible Death Benefit: Universal Life Insurance policies offer the option to adjust the death benefit, providing policyholders with the ability to increase or decrease the benefit amount as their coverage needs change over time. This flexibility is subject to insurability and policy guidelines, which will be detailed here.

Cash Value Component. Like whole life insurance, universal life plans feature a cash value component that increases with time in accordance with the interest that the insurer credits. This segment will delve into how the interest rate is determined, the impact of market conditions, and the options policyholders have for using the cash value.

Understanding the Interest Rate Mechanism

Fixed vs. Variable Interest Rates: This part will explore the differences between policies that offer a fixed interest rate on the cash value versus those that provide a variable rate tied to market performance, including the risks and rewards associated with each.

Minimum Guaranteed Interest Rate: The cash value of a universal life insurance policy will rise at least as fast as the market does, thanks to the policy's minimum guaranteed interest rate. This text will examine the importance of this guarantee in ensuring the protection of the policy's cash value.

The Pros and Cons of Universal Life Insurance

Advantages
- **Flexibility:** Policyholders may customize their coverage as their financial circumstances change thanks to the flexibility to modify the death benefit and premiums.
- **Growth Potential:** The cash value of a UL policy has the potential to grow more significantly than that of a Whole Life policy, especially in favorable market conditions.
- Transparency: UL policies offer greater transparency in the cost structure, allowing policyholders to see where their premiums are going.

Disadvantages
- **Complexity:** The flexibility and adjustable aspects of UL insurance can make it more complex to manage and understand.
- **Interest Rate Risk:** Interest rate fluctuations affect the increase of the cash value, which can impact the policy's value and the need for higher premiums in the future.
- **Costs:** The cost of insurance can increase as the policyholder ages, potentially requiring higher premiums to maintain the policy.

Navigating the Choices

Assessing Your Financial Goals
Identifying your long-term financial objectives is vital when considering a Universal Life Insurance policy. This section will guide potential policyholders on aligning their insurance choices with their financial plans and the importance of flexibility and growth potential in their decision-making process.

Comparing UL Policies: Not all Universal Life Insurance policies are equally created. This part will cover the key factors to compare when evaluating different UL policies, including the cost of insurance charges, premium flexibility, interest crediting rates, and the strength of the insurance company.

Working with a Financial Advisor: Given the intricate and subtle characteristics of UL insurance, it is strongly advised to seek guidance from a financial counselor or insurance expert. This segment will stress the importance of professional guidance in choosing a UL policy that best fits one's needs and financial situation.

Universal Life Insurance in Your Financial Portfolio

A key part of an all-encompassing financial plan, universal life insurance provides a special blend of flexibility, growth potential, and lifetime coverage. For those seeking adaptable insurance coverage that can evolve with their life changes, Universal Life Insurance provides a solution that balances security with economic freedom.

Overview of Variable Universal Life Insurance

Variable universal life insurance (VUL) is a kind of permanent life insurance policy that offers investors the chance to build wealth while still receiving the protections of universal life insurance. With this kind of insurance, the policyholder may invest a part of their premium money in a variety of financial products, like bonds, stocks, and mutual funds. Here is a deeper look at the unique features, advantages, and things to think about with variable universal life insurance.

Your universal life insurance policy's cash value may be used in a number of ways in addition to providing lifelong coverage. The flexibility of premium payments and the ability to choose where the cash value is invested make VUL policies particularly appealing to individuals looking for an insurance product that also serves as a financial investment tool.

Key Features of VUL

Investment Component: One of the defining features of VUL is its investment component, The insurance company offers policyholders a number of investment options from which they may choose to put the cash worth of their investments. This could increase the cash value more significantly than the guaranteed interest rate provided by universal life policies or traditional whole-life.

Flexible Premiums: VUL plans allow adjustable premium payments, much like universal life insurance. In times of financial hardship or windfall, policyholders have the ability to modify the premiums they pay into their plans, subject to certain limitations.

Adjustable Death Benefit: Policyholders can adjust the death benefit, allowing them to increase or decrease the amount of coverage as their financial situation or insurance needs change over time.

Potential Benefits

Growth Potential: The investment options available within a VUL policy can offer higher growth potential for the cash value component compared to traditional life insurance policies. This is especially appealing to those who have a longer investment timeframe and a greater willingness to take on risk.

Tax Advantages The cash value of VUL policies grows tax-deferred, and recipients get tax-free death payments. These tax benefits are shared by other forms of life insurance.

Financial Flexibility The life insurance policy's variable premium payments and adjustable death benefit provide a unique amount of financial flexibility that is not often available in other kinds of plans.

Considerations and Risks

Market Risk: The investment component of VUL policies carries inherent market risk. Poor investment performance can lead to a decrease in the cash value, potentially requiring higher premium payments to maintain the policy.

Investment Management: Policyholders need to actively manage their investment selections within the policy or seek professional management, adding a layer of complexity and requiring a more hands-on approach.

Costs and Fees: VUL policies often have higher costs and fees, including management fees for investment options, mortality and expense charges, and administrative fees. These costs can reduce investment returns and decrease the policy's cash value.

Choosing a VUL Policy

Assessing Your Risk Tolerance: Prospective VUL policyholders should thoroughly evaluate their capacity to handle risk and their current financial circumstances. The appeal of investment growth must be balanced against the risk of market volatility.

Understanding the Investment Options. It's crucial to understand the range of investment options offered within a VUL policy, including their historical performance, risk level, and management fees.

Long-term Strategy: Consider how a VUL policy fits into your long-term financial strategy, including retirement planning, estate planning, and tax implications.

Consult with a Professional: Speak with a financial counselor or insurance expert is advised due to the intricacy and hazards involved with VUL coverage. To determine whether VUL insurance fits your risk tolerance and financial objectives, they may provide assistance.

Variable Universal Life Insurance provides a unique blend of life insurance coverage and investment opportunities. While it provides an opportunity for cash value growth and financial flexibility, it also requires careful consideration of the associated risks and costs. For those with the risk tolerance and financial acumen to manage their investments, a VUL policy can be a valuable component of a comprehensive financial plan.

Final Expense Coverage

Among life insurance options, last expenditure coverage stands out as a considerate way to ease the burden of saying goodbye. To help ease the financial burden on families, this insurance policy covers expenses linked to end-of-life care, including funeral costs, medical bills, and any outstanding debts. Getting last expenditure insurance, sometimes called burial or funeral insurance, is a simple and easy way to make sure that your last desires are met. respected without putting undue financial burden on family and friends

Key Features of Final Expense Insurance

Guaranteed Acceptance: The assured acceptance policy of last expenditure insurance is one of its most attractive features. Usually, this insurance policy does not need a medical examination, making it a suitable option for persons with health conditions that may exclude them from other forms of life insurance.

Fixed Premiums: Final expenditure plans typically provide the advantage of fixed premiums, ensuring that the payment amount is stable over the term of the policy. This predictability allows for easier financial planning, ensuring that coverage remains uninterrupted.

Moderate Coverage Amounts
Designed to cover specific end-of-life expenses, final expense insurance policies generally offer moderate coverage amounts. This targeted coverage helps to keep premiums affordable while providing sufficient funds to cover funeral and burial costs, which can be significant.

The Importance of Final Expense Insurance

Easing the Burden on Families: The death of a loved one presents an intensely tough period, typically complicated by the burden of financial responsibilities. Final expense insurance offers peace of mind, knowing that funeral expenses and other final debts will not add to the family's burdens during a period of mourning.

Planning for the Inevitable: Final expense insurance encourages individuals to plan for the inevitable, allowing for personal preferences regarding funeral arrangements to be honored. This proactive approach ensures that one's final wishes are respected and can significantly ease the decision-making process for family members.

Streamlined and Accessible: The simplicity and accessibility of final expense insurance make it a practical option for many, particularly for older adults or those with health concerns. The streamlined application process and absence of medical exams remove barriers to obtaining coverage, ensuring more individuals have access to this vital financial resource.

Considerations When Choosing Final Expense Insurance

Assessing Coverage Needs: It's crucial to evaluate the anticipated costs of final expenses to choose a policy with adequate coverage. Considerations should include funeral service preferences, the cost of a burial plot or cremation, and any debts or medical bills that may be left behind.

Comparing Policies: Not all final expense policies are created equal. It is vital to compare offerings from various insurers, paying close attention to premium costs, coverage limits, and policy terms. Reading the fine print can reveal differences that significantly impact a policy's value and suitability.

Consulting with Financial Advisors: Financial advisors and insurance agents may help those who aren't sure what to look for in a last expenditure coverage. These professionals can guide you through the process of selecting insurance and making sure it fits in with your overall financial plan.

Final expense coverage stands out as a thoughtful approach to planning for the inevitable, offering a mechanism to protect loved ones from financial stress during a time of loss. This type of insurance embodies a considerate and proactive stance towards end-of-life planning, ensuring that final wishes are carried out with dignity and without imposing an undue burden on those left behind. As such, final expense insurance is not just about financial planning; it's a final act of care and consideration for one's family, ensuring peace of mind for all involved.

Understanding Provisions in Life Insurance Policies

Navigating through the intricacies of life insurance policies can sometimes feel like a journey through a labyrinth, with provisions acting as the guiding signs. These provisions – clauses, terms, and conditions embedded in an insurance contract – define the policy's operating rules, protections, and the mutual obligations of the insurer and the insured. Understanding these provisions is crucial for policyholders to grasp the extent of their coverage, the limitations, and the specific circumstances under which benefits are payable.

Standard Provisions in Life Insurance

The Incontestability Clause: This provision is a promise by the insurer that after a certain period, typically two years, they cannot contest the policy's validity due to misstatements by the insured, except under cases of fraud. This clause protects beneficiaries from the risk of claim denial due to honest mistakes or omissions in the application process.

Suicide Clause: Life insurance contracts sometimes include a suicide clause, which stipulates that if the insured person takes their own life within a certain timeframe from when the policy starts, generally two years, the death benefit will not be disbursed. Alternatively, the insurer may just reimburse the premiums that have been paid up until now.

Grace Period: The grace period provision allows policyholders a specified time, usually 30 days, to pay an overdue premium without causing the policy to lapse. This period ensures coverage continuity despite minor payment delays.

Misstatement of Age or Sex: This provision addresses the impact of incorrect information regarding the insured's age or sex on the policy. If such a misstatement is discovered, Policy benefits may be adjusted by the insurer to match what the premiums would have bought at the appropriate age or sex.

Policy Loans: Policies that include a cash value component, like whole life insurance, have a clause that allows the policyholder to borrow money using the policy's cash value as collateral. This provision governs the loan interest rates, repayment terms, and effects on the death benefit.

Beneficiary Designation: This crucial provision allows the policyholder to name one or more beneficiaries to receive the policy's death benefit. Policyholders are also given the flexibility to change beneficiaries unless the designation is irrevocable.

Accelerated Death Benefit: This provision allows the insured to receive a portion of the death benefit under specific conditions before death, such as a terminal illness diagnosis. It provides financial relief when it's most needed, although it reduces the benefit ultimately paid to beneficiaries.

Special Provisions and Riders

Waiver of Premium Rider: In the case that the policyholder becomes totally disabled and unable to work, this rider enables the insurer to maintain the policy without additional payments from the policyholder.

Guaranteed Insurability Rider: This provision gives the policyholder the ability to get supplementary coverage at specified future dates or significant life events without the need for extra medical evaluation, guaranteeing that the insured may enhance their coverage in response to life changes.

Navigating Policy Exclusions

Life insurance policies also have exclusions and circumstances under which they will not pay out. Common exclusions include deaths from risky activities, certain natural disasters, or acts of war. Understanding these exclusions is as important as understanding the coverage provisions.

Life insurance provisions are the backbone of the contract between the insured and the insurer. They detail the policy's scope, limitations, and mechanisms for addressing various situations during the policy's term. Thoroughly understanding these provisions ensures that policyholders can make informed decisions and plan for the future with clarity and confidence. As life insurance is a cornerstone of financial planning, Acquiring this information enables people to personalize their insurance according to their unique requirements and life situations, guaranteeing sufficient protection for themselves and their loved ones.

Riders in Life Insurance Policies

Riders in life insurance policies are akin to customizing a vehicle to meet specific needs and preferences. Just as one might add all-wheel drive for better performance in rugged terrain, insurance riders add flexibility and additional benefits to a standard life insurance policy. In addition to the necessary financial security, policyholders may rest easy knowing they can personalize their coverage with these extra benefits.

Common Riders in Life Insurance

Waiver of Premium Rider This rider guarantees the uninterrupted continuation of the policyholder's insurance coverage in the event of complete disability and inability to work, without requiring the payment of premiums. It's a safeguard ensuring that one's life insurance protection remains intact during challenging times, maintaining the policy's benefits without further financial burden.

Guaranteed Insurability Rider: As life circumstances evolve, the need for extra life insurance may also vary. The Guaranteed Insurability Rider enables policyholders to get supplementary coverage at designated intervals without the need for extra medical examinations or demonstrating insurability. This rider is especially advantageous as it guarantees the capacity to expand coverage in light of life events like substantial increases in income, marriage, or having children.

Accidental Death Benefit Rider: This rider, which goes by the name "double indemnity," adds to the death benefit of the basic policy in the event that the insured's untimely demise is the consequence of an accident. It's a way to ensure that beneficiaries have extra financial support in the sudden loss of a loved one due to unforeseen circumstances.

Child Term Rider The Child Term Rider offers transient life insurance coverage for the offspring of the insured. This rider normally provides a limited amount of coverage that may be converted into permanent life insurance when the kid becomes an adult, without the need for a medical examination.

Critical Illness Rider If an individual is diagnosed with a certain severe disease, this rider offers a one-time payment that may be used for medical bills, living expenses, or any other financial need. The Critical Illness Rider acts as a financial cushion, offering support during a challenging time when the focus should be on recovery and well-being.

Long-Term Care (LTC) Rider With healthcare costs rising, particularly for long-term care services, this rider addresses a significant concern for many. A policyholder may utilize the LTC Rider to pay for long-term care expenses out of their death benefit, for example, nursing facility costs or in-home care while safeguarding savings and retirement assets for other purposes.

Choosing the Right Riders

When assessing riders, it is essential to analyze individual and familial requirements, financial objectives, and the precise conditions of each rider. It's essential to ruminate the cost of riders, which is usually included in the policy's premium, in relation to the possible advantages and sense of security they provide.

Review and Adjust as Needed

It is crucial to periodically reassess and modify life insurance coverage and riders as life circumstances change, as the insurance requirements may vary over time. major life milestones, i.e., getting married, having a kid, or achieving major job progress, may need a reassessment of one's life insurance plan.
Riders add a layer of customization to life insurance policies, allowing policyholders to adapt their coverage to meet specific needs and concerns. Whether it's securing financial stability for one's family in the face of adversity, ensuring the ability to increase coverage as life changes, or providing for special care needs,

riders offer a flexible solution to enhance life insurance protection. By carefully selecting riders that align with personal and financial objectives, individuals can achieve a comprehensive insurance plan that offers reassurance and security for the future.

Options in Life Insurance Policies

Life insurance policies aren't just about paying premiums and securing a death benefit; they're also about the options that empower policyholders to adapt their coverage to fit changing life situations. These options, integral components of a life insurance contract, provide flexibility and control, allowing policyholders to make adjustments over time that align with their evolving personal circumstances and financial goals.

Key Options in Life Insurance

Conversion Option A term life insurance policy's conversion option is crucial. With this feature, policyholders may convert their term insurance to permanent coverage without needing a fresh medical examination or evidence of insurability. It's a lifesaver for those who want to keep their coverage even if their health changes throughout the policy.

Policy Loan Option Both whole life and universal life insurance policies have a cash value element that increases gradually as time passes. When needed, the policyholder's cash value may be used as collateral for a loan under the policy loan option, providing financial flexibility. You may employ loans against the cash value of the insurance for any reason, such as supporting retirement plans, paying for schooling, or even emergency costs.

Dividend Options Some types of permanent life insurance, particularly participating whole life insurance policies issued by mutual insurance companies, may earn dividends. Dividends, while not guaranteed, can be used in various ways according to the policyholder's choice: In order to get supplementary insurance, lower insurance payments, accrue interest, or even obtain cash. Policyholders have the ability to customize the policy's growth or cost management to match their evolving demands.

Surrender Option Policyholders have the option to surrender their policies before they mature or the insured passes away. Upon surrender, the policyholder receives the cash surrender value, a sum that may be lower than the total premiums paid but can deliver instant liquidity. It's essential to reflect the long-term implications of surrendering a policy, as this action terminates the coverage and may have tax implications.

Automatic Premium Loan Option Designed as a safety net, the automatic premium loan option helps prevent a policy from lapsing due to non-payment of premiums. This option ensures that the insurance remains active by automatically borrowing against the cash value to pay the premium if it is not paid within the grace period. This option requires sufficient cash value to cover the premiums and is particularly useful in maintaining coverage during financial hardships.

Choosing and Managing Your Policy Options

Understanding and selecting the suitable options for your life insurance policy requires a cautious evaluation of your potential future needs, current financial situation, and long-term financial goals. Here are some steps to effectively manage your policy options:

Regular Review It is vital to periodically assess your policy and its alternatives to make sure they continue to match your changing life circumstances and financial objectives. This may involve adjusting coverage, converting a term policy, or utilizing policy dividends differently.

Professional Guidance Understanding the intricacies of life insurance choices may be difficult. Getting help from an insurance specialist may give valuable views and specific solutions, guaranteeing that you make well-informed choices about your policy alternatives.

Informed Decision-Making Before exercising any option within your policy, consider the long-term implications, potential costs, and benefits. Informed decision-making is critical to maximizing the value of your life insurance coverage and ensuring it continues to meet your financial security needs.
Options within life insurance policies provide a framework for customization and adaptability, empowering policyholders to make adjustments that reflect their changing life situations and financial goals. By understanding and thoughtfully managing these options, you can ensure your life insurance coverage remains a dynamic component of your overall financial plan, providing security and comfort for you and your family.

Exclusions in Life Insurance Policies

Whole life insurance policies promise peace of mind and financial protection; it's essential to recognize that this promise comes with specific boundaries, known as exclusions. These exclusions are particular conditions or circumstances under which the policy will not pay out the death benefit. Understanding these limitations is crucial for policyholders to have a clear view of the coverage scope and to manage expectations regarding the policy's benefits.

Standard Exclusions in Life Insurance

Suicide Exclusion Life insurance contracts sometimes have a suicide exclusion provision, stipulating that if the policyholder takes their own life within a certain timeframe, generally two years after the commencement of the policy, Insurance company refuses to pay death benefit. Instead, the insurer may only return the premiums paid to the policy's beneficiaries. This exclusion aims to prevent the misuse of life insurance for financial gain from such tragic circumstances.

Contestability Period Not an exclusion per se, the contestability period is a time frame, often the first two years of the policy, during which the insurer can investigate and deny claims based on misrepresentations or omissions made during the application process. In the event of the insured's death within this time frame, the insurer retains the right to verify the correctness of the application, potentially leading to a claim denial if inaccuracies or fraud are discovered.

Dangerous Activities or Hobbies Many life insurance policies exclude deaths resulting from engagement in certain dangerous activities or hobbies, such as skydiving, mountaineering, or car racing. These exclusions are based on the increased risk associated with these activities. Policyholders involved in such hobbies may need to seek additional coverage or specific riders that cover these risks.

War and Military Service Some life insurance policies might exclude deaths resulting from terrorism, military service, or war. Given the high-risk nature of such circumstances, insurers often exclude these situations to mitigate their risk exposure. Individuals in the military or those traveling to war-torn regions should carefully review their policies for these exclusions and consider additional coverage if necessary.

Illegal Activities Life insurance plans often do not provide coverage for fatalities that occur as a consequence of the insured person's involvement in illicit activities or the commission of a crime. This exclusion underscores the principle that life insurance is not intended to provide rewards or benefits derived from unlawful conduct.

Alcohol and Substance Abuse Deaths attributable to alcohol or substance abuse may also be excluded under the terms of a life insurance policy. If the insured's death is directly related to the abuse of drugs or excessive alcohol consumption, the insurer may deny the death benefit claim based on this exclusion.

Navigating Policy Exclusions

Careful Review and Consultation Understanding the exclusions in your life insurance policy is essential. Talk to your insurance agent and read your policy details thoroughly to clarify any questions or concerns you may have about specific exclusions.

Disclosure and Honesty Full disclosure and honesty during the application process are crucial to avoid issues related to exclusions, especially during the contestability period. Ensure all information is accurate and complete to prevent future complications with claim denials.

Consider Additional Coverage For those engaged in high-risk activities or with specific needs not covered by a standard life insurance policy, considering additional coverage options or specialized riders that address these exclusions is advisable.

Exclusions in life insurance policies delineate the boundaries of coverage, ensuring policyholders are aware of the specific circumstances under which the death benefit would not be payable. By comprehending these exceptions, folks may make well-informed choices about their life insurance policy, guaranteeing that their financial planning is in line with their lifestyle and the welfare of their dependents.

Retirement Planning with Life Insurance Policies

Retirement planning is a crucial aspect of financial security, encompassing various strategies and products to ensure a comfortable and secure life post-retirement. Life insurance policies, often associated primarily with death benefits, also offer significant advantages for retirement planning. By integrating life insurance into retirement strategies, individuals can leverage these policies for income, savings, and legacy planning.

The Role of Life Insurance in Retirement Planning

Life insurance policies, particularly those with a cash value component, can play a multifaceted role in retirement planning. Beyond their fundamental purpose of providing a death benefit, certain types of life insurance can accumulate cash value over time, offering a potential source of retirement income.

Whole Life Insurance It offers continuous coverage throughout one's lifetime, along with the advantage of a cash value account that increases at a guaranteed pace. Policyholders can use this cash value as a tax-advantaged savings vehicle, borrow against it, or even withdraw funds during retirement.

Universal Life Insurance It provides the option to customize premium payments and modify the amount of the death benefit. Additionally, it has a cash value element that increases in accordance with the policy's interest rate. Policyholders can manage the policy to prioritize cash value growth, which can then be used to supplement retirement income.

Variable Universal Life Insurance It enables policyholders to allocate the cash value of the policy into several investment possibilities, providing the opportunity for increased growth potential. This growth, subject to market risks, can significantly enhance retirement savings if managed wisely.

Strategies for Utilizing Life Insurance in Retirement

Supplementing Retirement Income Life insurance plans provide the option to access the cash value via loans or withdrawals, which may serve as an additional source of income during retirement. This approach can be particularly advantageous because policy loans are typically tax-free.

Estate Planning and Legacy Building Because life insurance provides a tax-efficient means of transferring money to heirs, it may be quite important when it comes to estate planning. This can ensure that retirement savings are preserved for the policyholder's enjoyment, with the insurance providing for heirs.

Long-Term Care Funding Certain life insurance plans include riders that let the insured use the death benefit to pay for long-term care expenditures due to the growing cost of these services. Making sure that long-term care requirements are met without depleting other retirement funds may be a critical part of retirement planning.

Tax Advantages Life insurance plans provide many tax benefits that might be advantageous for retirees. The increase in cash value is not subject to immediate taxation, and if handled correctly, policy loans and withdrawals may be exempt from taxes. This makes life insurance an efficient tool for retirement planning.

Considerations and Limitations

Although there are some significant drawbacks and concerns to bear in mind, whole life insurance may be a useful instrument for retirement planning:

- **Costs and Fees:** Life insurance policies, especially those that offer cash value growth and investment options, come with costs and fees that can impact the policy's overall value and the available retirement income.
- **Investment Risks:** Policies that involve investment components, like variable universal life insurance, carry risks associated with market fluctuations, which can affect the cash value and retirement income.
- **Policy Management**: Effective use of life insurance in retirement planning requires careful management of the policy, particularly in terms of premium payments, cash value growth, and ensuring the policy remains in force.

Integrating life insurance into retirement planning can offer significant benefits, from providing a supplementary source of retirement income to facilitating estate planning and delivering long-term care solutions. However, leveraging life insurance for retirement requires a strategic approach, taking into account the costs, management, and potential risks involved. With careful planning and consideration, life insurance can be a powerful component of a comprehensive retirement strategy, ensuring financial security and peace of mind in the golden years.

Taxation in Life Insurance Policies

In order to maximize benefits while minimizing tax burden, policyholders must be aware of the tax ramifications related to life insurance contracts. This section delves into the various aspects of taxation within life insurance, providing insights into how these financial tools interact with tax laws.

Premium Payments

Generally, premium payments for life insurance policies are made with after-tax dollars, meaning they are not tax-deductible. If the policyholder is also the insured, then this rule does not apply to their own life insurance. But there are certain life insurance plans that are specialized to businesses that are an exception to this rule, where premiums might be deductible as a business expense under specific conditions.

Death Benefit Payouts

The tax treatment of death benefit payments is a very appealing aspect of life insurance. Beneficiaries do not often have to pay federal income tax on death benefits after the covered individual has passed away. This tax exemption applies regardless of the policy size, providing a significant advantage in planning for financial legacy and security.

Exceptions and Considerations
- **Estate Taxes:** In the case of large estates, the amount of the death benefit may be included as part of the estate for estate tax purposes, particularly if the policyholder was the owner of the policy. Effective estate planning may assist reduce possible estate taxes.
- **Interest Payments:** If a death benefit is paid out in installments and includes interest, the interest portion may be taxable as income to the beneficiary.

Cash Value Growth

There is a tax-free accumulation of cash value in permanent life insurance plans, such as universal life and whole life. What's more, policyholders aren't taxed on the interest, dividends, or capital gains that accumulate within the policy's cash value, so the compounding effect increases over time.

Withdrawals and Loans
- **Withdrawals:** The standard tax-free withdrawal limit is the amount of premiums put into the insurance, also known as the basis. Withdrawals that go over the base, nevertheless, can end up being considered income.
- **Loans:** As long as the insurance is still in effect, the loan from the policy is not considered income. Any amount borrowed over the policy's base that remains after the insurance expires or is surrendered can be subject to taxation.

Policy Surrender

Redeeming a permanent life insurance policy for its cash value may result in tax consequences. The policyholder may incur taxes on the surplus of the cash surrender value exceeding the premiums put into the policy (known as the policy's basis), which will be considered regular income.

Policy Exchanges

If certain requirements are satisfied, policyholders may swap one life insurance policy for another under Section 1035 of the Internal Revenue Code without facing immediate tax repercussions. This provision allows policyholders to adapt their financial planning without incurring tax liabilities from the exchange. A few benefits of life insurance plans' tax status include tax-free death payouts and tax-deferred cash value growth. However, due to the complexity of life insurance taxes, significant preparation and thought are required. Policyholders should consult with tax professionals or financial advisors to understand and navigate the tax implications of their policies, ensuring they align with their broader financial and estate planning goals.

Other Life Insurance Considerations

Navigating the world of life insurance involves more than just understanding the types of policies, riders, and exclusions. Several other vital considerations can impact your decision-making process, the effectiveness of your coverage, and how you manage your policy over time. This section delves into some of these critical aspects to give you a well-rounded perspective on life insurance.

Policy Review and Adjustments

Life insurance is not a product that can be left unattended or neglected. As your circumstances evolve, your need for life insurance also varies. Frequently evaluating your policy guarantees that your insurance coverage matches your present living circumstances. Significant life events such as marriage, the arrival of a child, a substantial work transition, or retirement may need modifications to your insurance coverage. Moreover, changes in your financial objectives, such as eliminating debt or acquiring a residence, might also influence your need for life insurance.

Beneficiary Designations

A life insurance policy's beneficiary designation is one of its most important features. In this section, you may choose the beneficiary of your policy's death benefit. It is crucial to ensure that these designations are regularly updated to accurately represent your current preferences. Modifications in family dynamics, such as matrimony, dissolution of marriage, or the demise of a previously assigned recipient, need adjustments to your policy to ensure that the intended beneficiaries get the death benefit.

Estate Planning and Life Insurance

One of the most important aspects of estate planning is life insurance. It can be utilised to distribute assets fairly among beneficiaries, pay estate taxes, or offer liquidity upon death. When structured properly, life insurance proceeds can be received by beneficiaries free of income tax or estate tax. Using life insurance in conjunction with trusts can also provide a means to manage how your assets are distributed to beneficiaries after your death.

Tax Implications

It's crucial to comprehend the tax ramifications of your life insurance coverage. A life insurance policy's death payout is normally tax-free for the beneficiaries; however, there may be tax implications for other uses of the policy, such as loans or cash value withdrawals. Though they may be a component of tax-advantaged plans, policies like whole life and universal life that accrue cash value must be properly negotiated to prevent unexpected tax obligations.

Financial Ratings and Insurer Selection

The first concern when selecting a life insurance policy is the financial robustness and stability of the chosen insurance provider. Fitch, Standard & Poor's, A.M. Best, and Moody's, are some of the rating organizations that offer information about an insurer's financial stability and claim payment capacity. If you want your beneficiaries to get the death benefit when the time comes, you should choose an insurer that is financially solid.

Policy Loans and Withdrawals

For policies with a cash value component, understanding the terms and conditions around policy loans and withdrawals is crucial. While accessing the cash value can provide financial flexibility, it's important to consider the impact on the death benefit and the potential tax implications. Mismanagement of policy loans and withdrawals can lead to unintended consequences, including policy lapse or a taxable event.

Cost of Insurance

The cost of insurance within a policy, especially in universal life policies, can vary and impact the policy's cash value. Being aware of how these costs are calculated and can change over time is important for managing a policy effectively. For policies where the cost of insurance increases with age, ensuring that the policy remains funded sufficiently to cover these costs is essential to maintain coverage.

Life insurance is a powerful tool in your financial arsenal, offering protection for your loved ones and playing a crucial role in your overall financial strategy. By considering these additional aspects of life insurance, you can make more informed decisions, tailor your coverage to meet your evolving needs, and utilize life insurance to its fullest potential. You should get guidance from a insurance expert or financial counselor to negotiate the intricacies of life insurance and its integration into your overall financial strategy.

FUNDAMENTALS OF HEALTH INSURANCE

Health insurance stands as a cornerstone in managing personal health and financial well-being. A contract is established between a person and an insurance provider, whereby the insurer promises to bear a part of the individual's medical expenditures in return for a premium. This chapter delves into the essentials of health insurance, aiming to demystify its components, the importance of having coverage, and the various types available to consumers.

Understanding Health Insurance

The Purpose of Health Insurance: Health insurance is specifically developed to provide financial security against exorbitant medical bills, guaranteeing that customers may use essential healthcare services without shouldering the whole financial load. It's a safety net that covers treatments, surgeries, prescription drugs, and sometimes even preventive care and check-ups, depending on the policy.

How Health Insurance Works
- Premium: This is the amount you pay, typically monthly, to have health insurance. It's payable even if you don't use any medical services.
- Deductible: The deductible refers to the amount of money that you personally cover for medical treatments prior to your health insurance commencing its coverage.
- Copayments and Coinsurance: Your portion of the expenses for a covered healthcare treatment is determined either as a fixed price (copayment) or as a percentage of the approved amount for the service (coinsurance) after you have already paid your deductible.
- Out-of-Pocket Maximum/Limit: The amount you will be required to pay throughout the insurance term (typically a year) for services that are covered. The insurance provider covers covered treatments in full after you reach this sum.

Types of Health Insurance Plans

Fee-for-Service (Indemnity Plans): Patients have more choice to pick their healthcare providers with standard fee-for-service plans, but they generally have more out-of-pocket payments and premiums.

Managed Care Plans: These plans provide its members with all-inclusive health care and incentives to utilize the network of providers inside the plan. They consist of:

- **Health Maintenance Organizations (HMOs):** Mandate that members use healthcare providers inside the network and choose a primary care physician who oversees the coordination of their treatment.
- **Preferred Provider Organizations (PPOs):** Allow more flexibility in selecting healthcare providers and don't require a primary care physician.
- **Point of Service (POS):** A PPO/HMO hybrid that allows you to choose your primary care physician of choice while still allowing you to visit out-of-network doctors at a premium cost.

- **High Deductible Health Plans (HDHPs) with Health Savings Accounts (HSAs)** HDHPs cost less but have larger deductibles. They may work in tandem with Health Savings Accounts (HSAs), which are tax-advantaged savings accounts intended to cover eligible medical costs, to support patient-directed healthcare.

Choosing the Right Health Insurance Plan

Choosing the best health insurance plan requires evaluating your financial status, healthcare requirements, and desire for provider choice flexibility. Consider factors like the plan's network, coverage for medications, and whether your current healthcare providers are in-network. Evaluating the cost versus benefits of each plan type is crucial in making an informed decision.

Importance of Health Insurance

Having health insurance is essential for several reasons:

- **Protects Your Finances:** Health insurance can save you from facing massive debt due to unexpected medical expenses.
- **Access to Preventive Care:** Many plans cover preventive services, which can detect health issues early when they're more treatable.
- **Improves Health Outcomes:** People with health insurance are more likely to visit a doctor when needed, leading to better health outcomes.

Understanding the fundamentals of health insurance is key to navigating the healthcare system and making informed decisions about your coverage. Regularly reassessing and modifying your health insurance coverage is essential to ensure that it remains suitable for your evolving healthcare requirements and financial circumstances. By selecting an appropriate health insurance policy, you may safeguard your physical well-being and financial stability, ensuring tranquility for both yourself and your family.

Health Maintenance Organization (HMO) Plans

Health Maintenance Organization (HMO) plans represent a cornerstone in the landscape of health insurance options, offering a blend of cost efficiency and coordinated care. These plans are specifically created to provide members with a wide variety of healthcare services via a network of providers who have agreed to give services to members according to the terms of the insurance contract. Understanding the structure, benefits, and limitations of HMO plans is crucial for anyone navigating their health insurance options.

Structure of HMO Plans

Network of Providers The foundation of an HMO plan is its network of healthcare providers, which includes doctors, hospitals, and other healthcare professionals. Members must use these network providers to receive coverage for their healthcare services, except in emergency situations. This network system is central to the HMO's ability to control costs and coordinate care.

Primary Care Physician (PCP) Members are required to choose a Primary Care Physician (PCP) from within the HMO network. The PCP serves as the member's main healthcare provider, overseeing and coordinating all aspects of the patient's medical care. For most specialist services and procedures, members need a referral from their PCP to ensure that all provided care is necessary and integrated.

Benefits of HMO Plans

Cost Efficiency One of the most appealing aspects of HMO plans is their cost efficiency. HMOs often have cheaper out-of-pocket expenses and premiums than other types of insurance. This is partly because the HMO can negotiate favorable terms with its network providers and more effectively manage the care its members receive.

Emphasis on Preventive Care HMOs typically emphasize preventive care to keep members healthy and avoid costly medical treatments. This may include routine check-ups, screenings, and vaccinations, often provided at low or no cost to the member. The focus on prevention aligns with the broader goal of maintaining the overall health of the membership base.

Coordinated Care The requirement to select a PCP and the need for referrals to see specialists foster a coordinated approach to healthcare. This coordination helps to ensure that care is appropriate, necessary, and efficiently delivered, reducing the risks of duplicated tests and conflicting treatments.

Limitations of HMO Plans

Restricted Provider Network The requirement to use providers within the HMO network can be a limitation for members who wish to see providers outside of the network. Out-of-network care is typically not covered except in emergencies, meaning members must be comfortable with the choice and quality of providers within the HMO

Referral Requirements The need for referrals to see specialists can be a hurdle for some members, requiring an extra step in the process to receive care. While this can ensure that specialist care is necessary, it can also delay treatment and add complexity to healthcare decisions.

Geographic Coverage HMO plans are often geographically limited to a certain area or network. For individuals who travel frequently or live in rural areas, accessing in-network care can be more challenging compared to plans with a broader network.

Choosing an HMO Plan

When considering an HMO plan, evaluate the plan's network of providers, the costs associated with premiums and out-of-pocket expenses, and how the plan's structure aligns with your healthcare needs. It's also important to consider your preferences regarding the choice of healthcare providers and the process for accessing specialized care.

Health Maintenance Organization plans to offer a cost-effective and coordinated approach to healthcare, making them a popular choice for many individuals. The emphasis on preventive care and the structured network of providers can contribute to improved health outcomes and controlled healthcare costs. However, the limitations associated with provider choice and geographic coverage are important considerations. Understanding the details of how an HMO plan works can help individuals make informed decisions about their health insurance, ensuring they choose a plan that best fits their needs and lifestyle.

Individual Health Insurance

It is a type of health coverage that a person buys for themselves or their family rather than obtaining coverage through an employer or a government program. People who are self-employed, jobless, or work for companies without health insurance would find this alternative quite helpful. Customers can better navigate their healthcare coverage options when they have a firm grasp of the ins and outs of individual health insurance.

Understanding Individual Health Insurance

What is Individual Health Insurance? Individual health insurance plans are policies purchased by individuals to cover themselves and their dependents. These plans are available for purchase directly from insurance companies, via a licensed insurance agent, or through the Health Insurance Marketplace created by the Affordable Care Act (ACA).

Coverage Options Individual health insurance plans exhibit significant variation in terms of their coverage, premiums, deductibles, and out-of-pocket payments. Most plans typically cover a wide range of benefits, including prescription drugs, Preventive and wellness services, laboratory services, mental health and drug use disorder services, hospitalization, maternity and newborn care, outpatient care, and pediatric services.

The Affordable Care Act and Individual Insurance

The ACA sometimes referred to as Obamacare, had a substantial effect on individual health insurance by creating health insurance exchanges, forbidding insurers from refusing coverage based on pre-existing illnesses, and mandating that all plans provide a defined list of essential health benefits.

Health Insurance Marketplaces The ACA established health insurance markets, often known as exchanges, which enable people to evaluate and acquire insurance coverage. These marketplaces also provide access to income-based subsidies that can lower the cost of premiums and out-of-pocket expenses for those who qualify.

Open Enrollment Period The ACA included a yearly Open Enrollment Period, during which consumers have the opportunity to acquire or modify their health insurance coverage via the marketplace. Individuals may also apply for Special Enrollment Periods if they undergo certain life changes, such as getting married, having a child, or losing their current health insurance.

Choosing an Individual Health Insurance Plan

- **Assess Your Healthcare Needs** Think about the regular medical checkups, prescription drugs, and treatments that you and your family need, as well as your chosen doctors and hospitals. This assessment will help determine the most suitable plan type and coverage level.
- **Compare Plan Types** Point of Service (POS), Exclusive Provider Organization (EPO), Preferred Provider Organization (PPO), and Health Maintenance Organization (HMO) plans are among the many options for individual health insurance. Each jurisdiction has distinct regulations regarding network providers, expenses that must be paid directly by the patient, and the prerequisites for obtaining a referral to see a specialist.
- **Understand Costs** Beyond the monthly premium, it's crucial to understand a plan's deductible, copayments, coinsurance, and out-of-pocket maximum. These details affect the overall cost of the plan and how you pay for care.
- **Check the Provider Network** Make sure the plan you are considering covers your chosen physicians, hospitals, and clinics. Higher out-of-pocket expenses may arise from using non-network providers.

The Role of Subsidies

Many individuals purchasing insurance through the ACA marketplace qualify for subsidies that lower the cost of premiums and out-of-pocket expenses. Eligibility for these subsidies is based on income and family size.

Individual health insurance offers a vital safety net for those without access to employer-sponsored or government-provided healthcare coverage. With the introduction of the ACA, more people have access to affordable health insurance with essential health benefits. When selecting an individual health plan, it's important to carefully assess your healthcare needs, compare plan options, and consider the financial implications of premiums, deductibles, and other costs. Understanding these elements will enable you to choose a plan that best meets your health and financial needs, ensuring that you and your family have access to quality healthcare.

Provisions in Health Insurance: A Comprehensive Overview

Health insurance policies are complex documents that outline the coverage, limitations, and rules governing the relationship between the insurer and the insured. Embedded within these documents are various provisions, which are essentially clauses or stipulations designed to clarify terms, protect both parties, and outline the operational mechanics of the policy. Understanding these provisions is crucial for policyholders to fully comprehend their rights, responsibilities, and the extent of their coverage. This chapter aims to dissect and explain the key provisions commonly found in health insurance policies.

Eligibility Provisions

Age and Enrollment Periods These clauses outline the age-based eligibility criteria for insurance coverage as well as the timeframes for enrollment. Events that meet certain requirements, including getting married, having a child, or losing health insurance, may start special enrollment periods.

Dependent Coverage Outlines the criteria for who qualifies as a dependent under the policy, which can include spouses, children up to a certain age, and sometimes extended family members under specific conditions.

Coverage Provisions

Essential Health Benefits Specifies the primary scope of benefits covered by the plan, typically encompassing pediatric services, preventive care, laboratory services, rehabilitation services, prescription drugs, mental health services, newborn and maternity care, hospitalization, emergency services, and outpatient care.

Pre-existing Conditions The policy's stance on covering pre-existing conditions is outlined. The Affordable Care Act (ACA) forbids most health insurance companies from denying coverage because of a person's pre-existing condition.

Network and Out-of-Network Services Describes the differences in coverage levels for services received from providers within the insurance plan's network compared to those outside of it. This provision is crucial for understanding potential out-of-pocket costs.

Preventive Services Outlines coverage for preventive services, such as vaccinations and health screenings, which are often covered without copayments or deductibles to encourage early detection and prevention of diseases.

Cost-sharing Provisions

Deductibles Specifies how much the policyholder must spend out of pocket before the insurance provider starts to reimburse them for their portion of the covered treatments.

Copayments and Coinsurance Specifies the amounts that the insured must pay as a share of the cost for covered services, such as a fixed amount (copayment) or a percentage (coinsurance).

Out-of-Pocket Maximum Caps the total amount policyholders are required to pay out of pocket for covered services within a policy period, after which the insurance company pays 100% of covered costs.

Renewal and Cancellation Provisions

Policy Renewal Outlines the terms under which the policy can be renewed, including any changes in premiums or benefits at the time of renewal.

Cancellation Policy Details the conditions under which either party (the insurer or the insured) can cancel the policy, including any required notice period and the process for cancellation.

Claim and Appeal Provisions

Claim Submission and Processing Describes the process for submitting claims for covered services, including time frames for submission, documentation requirements, and how the insurer processes claims.

Appeals Process Outlines the procedure for appealing denied claims or coverage decisions, including the steps to file an appeal, the timeline for receiving a decision, and the rights of the insured during the appeal process.

Exclusions and Limitations Specifies the services and conditions that are not covered by the policy, as well as any limits on coverage, such as annual or lifetime caps on certain types of care.

Health insurance provisions play a critical role in defining the scope and limitations of coverage. By comprehensively grasping these clauses, policyholders may more effectively navigate their health coverage, make well-informed choices about their treatment, and optimize the advantages of their health insurance policy. It is crucial for people to thoroughly examine their unique policy paperwork and get guidance from insurance experts in order to explain any doubts since health insurance policies and laws might differ significantly.

Riders in Health Insurance: Enhancing Coverage and Flexibility

Riders are crucial in the domain of health insurance since they allow policyholders to tailor and improve a basic policy to suit their individual requirements. Riders are supplementary benefits that may be acquired and appended to a fundamental health insurance policy, providing coverage for ailments or treatments that are not included in the main plan. By comprehending the many categories of policyholders that are accessible and their operational mechanisms, persons may make well-informed choices to guarantee all-inclusive health insurance.

Types of Health Insurance Riders

Critical Illness Rider This rider offers a one-time payment if the insured person is diagnosed with a certain catastrophic disease, for example stroke, heart attack, or cancer. The funds can be used for various purposes, including treatment costs, daily expenses, or any financial needs arising during the recovery period, offering financial relief during a challenging time.

Accidental Death and Dismemberment (AD&D) Rider The Accidental Death and Dismemberment (AD&D) rider provides supplementary insurance coverage in the case of accidental death or specified injuries caused by an accident. This insurance policy normally provides a one-time payment for the accidental death of the insured person and may also cover different amounts of compensation for the loss of limbs, vision, or other permanent disabilities.

Hospital Cash Rider Also known as a hospital indemnity rider, this provides a daily cash benefit for each day the insured is hospitalized. The funds can help cover incidental expenses, such as transportation and food, that are not directly related to medical treatment.

Maternity Rider Designed to cover prenatal, delivery, and postnatal care, the maternity rider is a valuable addition for those planning to start or expand their family. Since standard health insurance plans may have limited or no maternity coverage, this rider ensures comprehensive care for mother and child.

Dental and Vision Riders These riders extend coverage to include dental and vision care, which are often not covered under basic health insurance policies. Dental riders may cover routine check-ups, cleanings, x-rays, and some procedures, while vision riders typically cover eye exams, glasses, and contact lenses.

Term Rider A term rider is a supplementary clause that adds a term life insurance component to a health insurance policy. This clause guarantees that recipients will receive a death benefit in the event that the covered person dies within the specified timeframe. This may provide an additional level of financial security for the policyholder's family.

Considerations When Choosing Riders

Assessing Your Needs Before adding riders to a health insurance policy, it's crucial to assess your and your family's healthcare needs, considering factors such as family medical history, lifestyle, and plans. This assessment helps determine which riders would provide the most benefit.

Cost vs. Benefit Analysis While riders can significantly enhance coverage, they also increase the overall cost of the insurance policy. It is essential to weigh the additional coverage benefits against the extra cost to ensure that the riders offer value and align with your financial capabilities.

Policy Terms and Conditions Understanding the specific terms, conditions, and limitations of each rider is essential. This includes knowing what is covered, any waiting periods before the coverage becomes effective, and the process for claiming benefits.

Review and Adjustment To make sure your health insurance keeps up with your ever-evolving demands, it's a good idea to evaluate and alter your riders on a regular basis. During policy renewal periods, consider whether any riders should be added, modified, or removed based on your current health status and coverage needs.
Riders in health insurance offer a mechanism to tailor standard health coverage to the specific needs of individuals and families, providing additional protection against a wide range of health-related financial risks. By carefully selecting riders based on a thorough assessment of needs and understanding the costs and benefits, policyholders can achieve a more comprehensive health insurance package that offers financial security and peace of mind. If you need help figuring out your health coverage alternatives or making a final selection, it's always a good idea to talk to an expert.

Options in Health Insurance

Health insurance policies often include a variety of options that allow policyholders to customize their coverage to better fit their needs and financial situations. These options can significantly impact the benefits you receive, how and when you receive care, and the overall cost of your insurance. Understanding these options is crucial for making informed decisions about your health coverage. Let's delve into some of the most common and impactful options available in health insurance policies.

Policy Upgrade Options Many health insurance plans offer the ability to upgrade your policy to include additional benefits or to increase the level of coverage for specific services. Upgrades might consist of better coverage for prescription drugs, lower deductibles, or access to a broader network of specialists. Upgrading your policy can lead to higher premiums, but it can also provide more comprehensive coverage and lower out-of-pocket costs for healthcare services.

Deductible Choices One of the primary ways you can tailor your health insurance policy is by choosing your deductible amount. The deductible refers to the amount of money that you personally contribute for healthcare services that are eligible for coverage, prior to your insurance plan commencing payment. Policies that have greater deductibles often have lower monthly rates, while policies with smaller deductibles are associated with higher premiums. Selecting the right deductible amount depends on your healthcare needs, financial situation, and risk tolerance.

Health Savings Account (HSA) Eligibility Certain health insurance policies are compatible with Health Savings Accounts (HSAs), which enable individuals to allocate funds on a pre-tax basis for the purpose of covering eligible medical costs. In order to qualify for an HSA, it is necessary to be enrolled in a high-deductible health plan (HDHP). Health Savings Accounts (HSAs) provide three-fold tax benefits: donations are eligible for tax deductions, the funds accumulate tax-free, and withdrawals utilized for approved medical costs are exempt from taxation.

Network Options Health insurance plans often operate within defined networks of hospitals, doctors, and other healthcare providers. Choosing a plan based on its network is crucial, especially if you have a preferred doctor or medical facility. Options typically include:

- **Health Maintenance Organization (HMO):** This type of organization requires members to seek care from providers within the network, except in emergencies, and usually requires referrals for specialists.
- **Preferred Provider Organization (PPO):** allows users more freedom in selecting providers and does not need expert references; but, going outside the network will increase prices.
- **Exclusive Provider Organization (EPO):** Like PPOs, however usually does not pay for any treatment received outside of the network outside of emergencies.
- **Point of Service (POS):** A cross between a PPO and an HMO, POS requires specialist referrals just like an HMO but permits out-of-network treatment at a premium much like a PPO.

Wellness Program Participation Many health insurers offer wellness programs that encourage healthy behaviors through various incentives. Participants may receive discounts on their premiums, gift cards, or reimbursements for gym memberships. Opting into these programs can not only lower your insurance costs but also promote better health and well-being.

Prescription Drug Coverage Tiers Prescription drug coverage is often structured in tiers, with each tier having a different cost associated with it. Lower tiers typically include generic drugs with the weakest copayments, while higher tiers cover brand-name or specialty drugs with higher copays or coinsurance. Understanding and utilizing this option can help manage medication costs effectively.

Telemedicine Services With the rise of digital health, many insurance plans now offer telemedicine services as an option. This allows you to consult with healthcare providers via phone or video call, often at a lower cost than in-person visits. Telemedicine can be a convenient and cost-effective option for non-emergency medical advice and treatment.

The options within health insurance policies provide a framework for customizing coverage to suit your individual health needs and financial situation. By meticulously evaluating each alternative and its compatibility with your healthcare preferences, you can customize your health insurance plan to provide the most suitable coverage that efficiently controls your healthcare expenses. It is important to get guidance from a health insurance expert or consultant in order to fully grasp the consequences of each choice and make well-informed judgments on your health insurance coverage.

Exclusions in Health Policies: Navigating the Boundaries

Understanding the exclusions in health insurance policies is essential for policyholders to navigate their coverage and avoid unexpected financial burdens effectively. Exclusions are specific conditions or circumstances under which a policy does not provide coverage. These restrictions are essential for risk management and cost control since they define the extent to which the insurance company is required to pay. Here's a detailed overview of common exclusions found in health insurance policies.

Pre-existing Conditions Several health insurance policies have clauses pertaining to pre-existing conditions, which refer to medical illnesses that were identified or treated prior to the commencement of a new insurance policy. While the Affordable Care Act (ACA) has placed substantial restrictions on insurance companies' capacity to refuse coverage for pre-existing conditions in individual and small group markets in the United States, there are still limitations, particularly in certain types of insurance like short-term health plans or travel insurance.

Cosmetic Procedures Health insurance typically does not cover procedures that are considered cosmetic, meaning those performed for aesthetic reasons rather than medical necessity. Examples include cosmetic surgery, hair transplants, and elective dental work that improves appearance but is not deemed medically necessary.

Experimental Treatments and Off-label Drug Use Treatments that are considered experimental or investigational are often excluded from coverage. This includes procedures, drugs, or therapies not widely accepted by the medical community or not approved by relevant regulatory agencies. Similarly, the use of approved drugs for off-label purposes (i.e., for conditions other than those for which the drug was approved) may not be covered.

Lifestyle Choices Health policies commonly exclude coverage for conditions or injuries resulting from confident lifestyle choices or behaviors deemed risky. This can include injuries sustained from high-risk recreational activities, such as skydiving, or health conditions resulting from substance abuse.

Non-Essential Services Services deemed non-essential or not medically necessary by the insurer may be excluded from coverage. This can encompass a range of services, including but not limited to routine foot care, adult dental services, and alternative therapies like acupuncture or homeopathy, depending on the specifics of the policy.

Travel Immunizations While preventive care, including vaccinations, is often covered under health insurance, immunizations required for international travel may not be. Policyholders planning to travel abroad should verify their coverage and may need to seek these immunizations out of pocket or through travel clinics.

Work-Related Injuries Injuries or illnesses that occur in the workplace are typically covered by workers' compensation insurance rather than personal health insurance. Consequently, most health policies exclude coverage for conditions that are compensable under workers' compensation or similar laws.

Understanding Your Policy Given the diversity of health insurance products available and the variability in individual policy terms, it is important for policyholders to thoroughly review and understand the exclusions in their health insurance plans. Knowing what is not covered is just as important as knowing what is covered. Policyholders may use this information to make educated choices on their extra coverage requirements, such as supplemental insurance policies, and plan financially for potential out-of-pocket healthcare costs.

Policyholders who are uncertain about the exclusions in their health insurance policy or how they apply should consult their insurance provider or a healthcare advisor. A clear understanding and proactive management of health coverage can prevent unexpected expenses and ensure that policyholders and their families receive the care they need without undue financial strain.

POLICY UNDERWRITING AND DELIVERY PROCEDURES

The process of obtaining health insurance involves several critical steps, from application through underwriting to the final delivery of the policy. This journey ensures that both the insurer and the insured understand the terms of the agreement, the coverage provided, and the obligations of each party. This chapter delves into the intricacies of policy underwriting and delivery procedures, shedding light on how insurance companies assess risk and decide on the terms of coverage.

Understanding Policy Underwriting

The Role of Underwriting Underwriting is the procedure by which insurers assess the level of risk associated with providing insurance coverage to a prospective policyholder. The process includes evaluating the individual's medical background, way of life, and other variables that may contribute to their risk level. Based on this evaluation, the insurer decides whether to offer coverage and, if so, at what premium rate.

Information Gathering The first step in underwriting is gathering information about the applicant. This may include:

- Medical history: A review of past and current health conditions, treatments, and outcomes.
- Lifestyle choices: Evaluation of habits such as tobacco use, alcohol consumption, and engagement in high-risk activities.
- Occupation and income: Understanding the applicant's job and income level can be relevant, especially for disability insurance underwriting.
- Age and gender: These demographic factors significantly influence risk assessment.

Risk Assessment Using the collected information, underwriters employ actuarial tables and statistical data to categorize applicants into risk classes. These classes determine the premiums that applicants will pay. Higher risk classifications typically result in higher premiums, reflecting the greater likelihood of the insurer needing to pay out claims.

The Delivery of the Policy

Issuance and Delivery Once underwriting is complete and the policy is approved, the insurer issues the policy documents and delivers them to the new policyholder. This package includes the policy itself, which outlines the terms of coverage, any riders or amendments added during underwriting, and a summary of benefits.

Review Period Policyholders are usually granted a review period during which they can read over their new policy to ensure it meets their needs and expectations. During this period, which often lasts 10 to 30 days, depending on the jurisdiction, If the policyholder decides the coverage isn't right for them, they may cancel and get their money back.

Effective Date of Coverage The policy documents will specify the effective date, which is when the insurance coverage begins. Policyholders must be aware of this date to understand when they are covered and to ensure they do not seek services thinking they are covered when the policy has yet to take effect.

Policy Amendments and Endorsements After the policy is issued, there may be situations where the policyholder needs to update or modify their coverage. This can be facilitated through policy amendments or endorsements, which are formal changes to the policy terms. Common reasons for amendments include adding or removing coverage options, changing beneficiary designations, or updating personal information.

Policyholder Responsibilities

Upon receiving their policy, policyholders have several responsibilities:

- **Thoroughly review the policy:** Ensure understanding of the coverage, limitations, exclusions, and their rights under the policy.
- **Pay premiums on time:** To keep the policy in force and avoid lapses in coverage.
- **Inform the insurer of changes,** Such as a new address, change in marital status, or other factors that might affect the policy or coverage.

An essential part of the health insurance system is the underwriting and distribution of policies. As a result, the insurer may continue to pay out to all of its customers despite more precise risk assessments and more personalized coverage. When people are well-versed in these processes, they are better able to understand their health insurance options and make educated judgments.

The Comprehensive Guide to the Health Insurance Underwriting Process

The underwriting process is a pivotal component in the health insurance industry. It determines the terms of coverage and premiums for applicants based on assessed risks. This detailed examination ensures that the insurer adequately understands the potential risk associated with insuring an individual or group. Here's an in-depth look at the underwriting process in health insurance, covering every aspect from the initial application to the final underwriting decision.

Initial Application

Submission of Personal Information The process begins when an applicant submits a health insurance application, providing detailed personal information. This includes age, gender, medical history, lifestyle habits (such as smoking or alcohol consumption), occupation, and any other factors that could influence health risks.

Health Questionnaires and Medical Exams The application process and the kind of insurance being considered by the insurer determine the requirements of the applicants to complete health questionnaires or undergo medical examinations. These exams could involve blood tests, blood pressure checks, and other diagnostic procedures to provide a current snapshot of the applicant's health.

Information Gathering

Review of Medical Records Insurers may request access to an applicant's medical records to verify the information provided in the application and to gain a more comprehensive understanding of the applicant's health history.

Prescription History Check A review of the applicant's prescription drug history can offer insights into their ongoing medical conditions and treatment plans, further informing the risk assessment.

Utilization of Third-Party Data Insurers often use data from third-party sources, such as the Medical Information Bureau (MIB), to cross-reference information provided by the applicant and identify any undisclosed medical conditions or risks.

Risk Assessment

Actuarial Analysis Using actuarial tables, insurers analyze the collected data to estimate the applicant's life expectancy and health risks. Actuaries consider factors like age, gender, and medical history to categorize applicants into risk classes.

Determination of Risk Class Applicants are assigned to a risk class based on the underwriting analysis. These classes range from preferred (lower risk) to standard (average risk) to substandard (higher risk), each affecting the policy's premium rates.

Policy Decision

Acceptance and Premium Calculation If the underwriting process concludes that the applicant can be insured, the insurer will accept the application and calculate the premium based on the risk class. Premiums are set to reflect the level of risk associated with insuring the applicant, with higher-risk individuals paying higher premiums.

Policy Riders or Exclusions In some cases, insurers may accept an application with specific riders or exclusions attached to the policy. These can limit coverage to particular conditions or activities deemed too risky to cover under standard terms.

Denial of Coverage In situations where the assessed risk is too high, insurers may deny coverage altogether. Denials are typically issued for severe or numerous health issues that significantly increase the risk beyond the insurer's acceptable threshold.

Policy Issuance and Delivery

The insurer will send the policy paperwork to the new policyholder when the underwriting procedure is finished and authorized. These documents outline the coverage terms, premiums, exclusions, and any riders attached to the policy.

Continuous Underwriting

Changes in Health Status or Lifestyle Policyholders are obligated to inform the insurer of any significant changes in health status or lifestyle that could affect their risk profile. Insurers may then reassess the policy terms based on this new information.

Policy Renewals At each renewal, insurers may review the policyholder's current health status and risk factors to adjust premiums or coverage terms accordingly. This ongoing underwriting process helps insurers manage risk over the life of the policy.

The underwriting process in health insurance is a meticulous and data-driven procedure designed to assess the risk of insuring applicants. By carefully evaluating personal and health information, insurers can set premiums that accurately reflect the risk they assume. Understanding this process helps applicants and policyholders navigate their health insurance options more effectively, ensuring they find coverage that meets their needs while being aware of the factors that influence their insurance costs and conditions.

Policy Issuance and Administration

After the underwriting process concludes with approval, the next crucial steps in an insurance policy's lifecycle are its issuance and subsequent administration. These stages are pivotal in transforming the underwriting decision into an active contract and maintaining the relationship between the insurer and the insured. This detailed note explores the intricacies of policy issuance and the ongoing administration tasks that ensure the policy remains accurate, up-to-date, and reflective of the agreement between both parties.

Policy Issuance

Finalizing the Policy Once underwriting approves the application, the insurer prepares the final policy documents. This includes incorporating any riders, endorsements, or adjustments made during underwriting. The policy document outlines the terms of coverage, including benefits, premiums, exclusions, and any conditions or obligations of the insured.

Policy Delivery The insurance company then delivers the policy to the new policyholder. Delivery methods can vary, including digital delivery via email, a secure online portal, or traditional postal service for physical documents. The delivery of the policy marks the official start of the insurance contract.

Acceptance and Review Period Upon receiving the policy, the insured is typically granted a review period, often referred to as a "free look" period, during which they can cancel the policy without penalty if they find the coverage unsatisfactory. This period is crucial for policyholders to understand their coverage fully and ensure it meets their expectations and needs.

Policy Administration

Premium Payments The policy's administration includes managing premium payments. Policyholders are responsible for making regular premium payments to keep the insurance coverage active. Insurers provide various payment options, including monthly, quarterly, semi-annual, or annual payments, and may offer methods like direct debit, online payments, or checks.

Updates and Changes Over time, policyholders may need to update personal information, change beneficiaries, or adjust coverage levels. Policy administration encompasses handling these requests, ensuring the policy reflects the current needs and circumstances of the insured.

Renewals and Modifications For term policies, administration includes managing renewals at the end of each term, if applicable. For permanent policies, there may be adjustments to premiums or benefits based on policy performance (e.g., in universal life policies). Insurers must communicate any changes or renewal options in a timely manner.

Claims Processing A critical component of policy administration is managing claims. Insurers establish procedures for filing claims, including documentation requirements and timelines. The administration process ensures that claims are processed efficiently, with clear communication to the insured about the status and outcome of their claim.

Customer Service and Support Effective policy administration relies heavily on customer service and support. Insurers assist various channels, including call centers, online portals, and in-person meetings with agents. Support includes answering questions, resolving issues, and providing guidance on policy features and services.

Compliance and Regulatory Reporting Insurers must adhere to regulatory requirements, including maintaining accurate records, reporting financial performance, and ensuring policies are issued and administered in compliance with laws and regulations. Policy administration includes these compliance tasks to protect both the policyholder and the insurer.

Policy issuance and administration are foundational to the functioning of the insurance industry, ensuring that policies accurately reflect the agreement between insurer and insured and that the needs of policyholders are met throughout the life of the policy. Effective administration fosters trust and satisfaction, which are crucial for maintaining long-term relationships with policyholders. By understanding these processes, policyholders can better navigate their coverage, ensuring they maximize the benefits of their insurance policy while staying informed and engaged with their insurer.

SOCIAL INSURANCE AND ADDITIONAL COVERAGE

Social insurance represents a cornerstone of modern social policy, providing a safety net that helps individuals navigate life's uncertainties. It complements individual insurance policies by covering aspects of risk that are widespread and difficult to manage on a personal basis. This chapter delves into the concept of social insurance, its various forms, and how it intersects with additional coverage options, offering a comprehensive understanding of its role in the broader insurance landscape.

Understanding Social Insurance

Definition and Purpose Social insurance is a government-sponsored program designed to provide financial protection against economic risks shared by many individuals, such as old age, disability, unemployment, and health issues. Unlike private insurance, where policies are individually underwritten, and premiums vary based on risk, social insurance programs typically require participation and contributions from all eligible individuals or employers, regardless of individual risk.

Key Characteristics

- Mandatory Participation: Most social insurance programs require participation by eligible individuals or employers, ensuring broad coverage and risk pooling.
- Defined Benefits: Benefits are typically predefined by law or regulation, offering predictability and stability to beneficiaries.
- Funded by Contributions: Employers, workers, or both may put money into programs; most often, payroll taxes do this.

Types of Social Insurance

Social Security Social Security programs in several nations provide monetary support to retired persons, handicapped individuals, and the dependents of dead workers. Benefits are based on the recipient's earnings record, with contributions collected through payroll taxes during their working years.

Unemployment Insurance Unemployment insurance provides those who lost their jobs due to circumstances beyond their control with short-term financial support. It aims to mitigate the economic impact of unemployment and facilitate re-entry into the workforce.

Disability Insurance Social disability insurance programs provide income support to individuals unable to work due to a disability. These programs help ensure that those who are physically or mentally incapacitated maintain a basic standard of living.

Health Insurance Government-funded healthcare programs, like the National Health Service (NHS) in the United Kingdom or Medicare in the United States, provide healthcare coverage to qualified groups, including the aged, handicapped, and, in some instances, low-income people.

Additional Coverage Options

Supplemental Insurance Individuals may opt for supplemental insurance policies to cover gaps in social insurance programs. These can include Medigap policies that cover Medicare copayments and deductibles, long-term care insurance, or supplemental unemployment insurance.

Private Disability Insurance While social insurance programs offer disability coverage, private disability insurance can provide additional benefits, broader coverage, and more flexibility in terms of benefit amounts and duration.

Critical Illness and Accident Insurance These insurance products offer lump-sum payments to individuals diagnosed with specific illnesses or who suffer from certain types of accidents, providing financial support above and beyond what social insurance programs offer.

The Interplay Between Social and Additional Insurance Coverage

Navigating the relationship between social insurance and additional coverage options requires understanding each's limitations and scope. Social insurance provides a basic level of protection, while additional coverage can tailor protection to individual needs, preferences, and financial situations. An informed approach involves assessing personal risk, financial goals, and the existing social insurance framework to determine the most appropriate and effective insurance strategy.

Social insurance plays a vital role in providing financial security and healthcare coverage to broad segments of the population, acting as a foundation upon which individuals can build additional coverage options. Understanding the nuances of social insurance and how it complements private insurance coverage is crucial for making informed decisions about personal and family protection strategies. By carefully navigating these waters, individuals can ensure comprehensive coverage that meets their needs and adapts to life's unpredictable challenges.

Social Security as a Type of Social Insurance

Social Security stands as a pivotal element within the realm of social insurance, designed to provide financial assistance to individuals during retirement, in the event of disability, or to surviving family members of deceased workers. This program embodies the principle of collective risk management, ensuring economic stability and support for its beneficiaries. This section delves into the intricacies of Social Security, exploring its origins, benefits, funding mechanisms, and the challenges it faces.

Origins and Purpose

Social Security was established in response to the economic vulnerabilities exposed by the Great Depression. Its primary aim was to secure a basic level of sustenance for older adults who, due to retirement or disability, could no longer earn a living through employment. Over the years, the program has expanded to include survivor benefits, disability insurance, and other social welfare functions, making it a comprehensive system of protection against loss of income due to age, disability, or death.

Types of Benefits

Retirement Benefits Workers may start collecting retirement benefits after they've paid into the Social Security system (via payroll taxes) and achieved the age of eligibility, which varies from 62 to 67 depending on the birth year. A worker's benefit amount is determined by taking their 35 highest-earning years and adjusting it for inflation.

Disability Benefits Social Security Disability Insurance (SSDI) offers payments to qualified employees who are unable to participate in significant and profitable employment owing to a medically verifiable physical or mental disability that is anticipated to last for a minimum of one year or lead to death. The determination of disability is strict, ensuring that only those genuinely unable to work receive benefits.

Survivors Benefits Survivor benefits are paid to the family members of deceased workers, including widows, widowers, and dependent children. These benefits are designed to help offset the loss of income resulting from the worker's death, providing financial support to those left behind.

Funding Mechanism

The primary source of funding for Social Security is derived from the collection of payroll taxes under the Federal Insurance Contributions Act (FICA). Both employers and workers contribute 6.2% of earnings, subject to a certain level. Self-employed persons are responsible for paying both shares. These funds are deposited into the Social Security Trust Funds and used to pay out current benefits, with any excess reserved for future payments.

Challenges and Sustainability

Demographic Shifts The aging population and declining birth rates present significant challenges to the sustainability of Social Security. As the ratio of workers paying into the system to beneficiaries receiving payouts decreases, the financial strain on the program increases.

Trust Fund Depletion Projections indicate that the Social Security Trust Funds could be depleted within the next few decades, potentially reducing the program's ability to pay full benefits. With legislative action to address this issue, future beneficiaries may avoid decreasing payments.

Reform Proposals Various proposals to ensure the long-term solvency of Social Security have been put forward, including increasing the retirement age, raising the cap on taxable earnings, adjusting the benefit formula, and enhancing revenue through higher payroll taxes. The debate over these proposals underscores the need for a balanced approach that preserves benefits while ensuring the program's financial health.

Social Security represents a foundational component of the social insurance framework, offering critical support to retirees, disabled workers, and survivors. Its role in providing financial stability and protecting against the economic impacts of aging, disability, and death is indispensable. However, addressing the challenges of demographic changes and trust fund sustainability is crucial for maintaining its effectiveness and reliability for future generations. As policymakers and the public grapple with these issues, the ongoing commitment to Social Security's core principles will be critical to its successful evolution and enduring legacy.

Unemployment Insurance

Unemployment insurance (UI) is an essential element of social insurance programs, offering temporary financial aid to those who have been unemployed due to circumstances beyond their control. It serves as an economic stabilizer and safety net, helping to cushion the financial blow of job loss for individuals and maintaining consumer spending during economic downturns. This section explores the structure, benefits, eligibility criteria, and challenges associated with unemployment insurance.

Structure and Purpose

Fundamentals of Unemployment Insurance While they look for new jobs, qualified workers may get some of their lost pay back via the federal-state program known as unemployment insurance. Financial support comes from employer taxes, which include FUTA levies at the federal level and jurisdiction-specific state taxes.

Goals of the Program The main objectives of unemployment insurance are to provide temporary economic support to those who are without employment, stabilize the economy during recessions by sustaining consumer spending, and encourage the jobless to quickly find new employment through various support services, such as job training and placement programs.

Benefits of Unemployment Insurance

Financial Assistance UI benefits offer crucial financial support, helping individuals to cover essential expenses for example healthcare, food, and housing, during periods of unemployment. The amount of the benefit typically depends on the recipient's previous earnings and the maximum limit set by the state.

Economic Stabilization By providing unemployed workers with financial assistance, UI benefits help to stabilize the economy during downturns by maintaining consumer spending. This, in turn, can prevent further job losses and support a quicker economic recovery.

Eligibility Criteria

Work and Earnings Requirements To qualify for unemployment insurance, individuals must meet specific work and earnings criteria during a base period. This ensures that only those who have demonstrated attachment to the workforce and contributed to the UI system through their employers are eligible.

Reason for Unemployment Eligibility for UI benefits requires that individuals have lost their jobs through no fault of their own, such as layoffs due to economic conditions or company closures. Those who quit without reasonable cause or are fired for misconduct are generally not eligible.

Availability and Job Search Recipients must be able and available to work and actively seek employment. Many states require beneficiaries to register with employment services and provide proof of their job search efforts to continue receiving benefits.

Challenges and Considerations

Funding and Solvency Issues The financial health of unemployment insurance funds can vary significantly by state, influenced by economic conditions, funding mechanisms, and benefit levels. Ensuring the solvency of UI funds, especially during periods of high unemployment, remains a persistent challenge.

Fraud and System Abuse Unemployment insurance systems are susceptible to fraud and abuse, including false claims and employer tax evasion. Strengthening integrity measures and modernizing UI systems are ongoing priorities to safeguard the program.

Disparities in Coverage Not all workers are covered by unemployment insurance, and eligibility criteria can exclude significant segments of the workforce, such as gig workers, freelancers, and part-time workers. Recent emergency measures, like the Pandemic Unemployment Assistance (PUA) program, have temporarily expanded coverage, highlighting discussions on permanent reforms.

In times of economic recession, unemployment insurance is an important safety net for those who have lost their jobs and for the economy as a whole. As the labor market evolves and new challenges emerge, ongoing discussions on how to adapt, fund, and administer the UI program are crucial to ensuring its continued effectiveness and sustainability. Addressing issues of solvency, fraud, and coverage disparities will be key to maintaining the UI program as a cornerstone of social insurance for future generations.

Disability Insurance

An integral part of any sound financial strategy should include disability insurance, which guarantees a steady flow of income in the event that a policyholder becomes disabled and unable to work. Whether resulting from injury, illness, or mental health conditions, disabilities can significantly impact an individual's earning capacity, leading to financial instability. This detailed note explores the facets of disability insurance, covering its importance, types, coverage details, eligibility criteria, and the claims process.

Importance of Disability Insurance

The risk of experiencing a disabling event is more common than many realize. Disability insurance serves as a safety net, ensuring that individuals maintain a stable income when they are unable to earn a living due to a disability. It helps cover everyday expenses and medical bills and maintains the individual's standard of living, reducing the financial strain on the individual and their family.

Types of Disability Insurance

Short-Term Disability Insurance (STD) STD policies provide benefits for short durations, typically ranging from a few weeks to several months. These policies are designed to cover temporary disabilities, such as those resulting from injuries or acute medical conditions, and often have a brief waiting period before benefits begin.

Long-Term Disability Insurance (LTD) LTD policies are used for longer-lasting disabilities, offering coverage that can last for several years or until the individual reaches retirement age. These policies typically have longer waiting periods, known as elimination periods, but provide more extended support for chronic or severe conditions.

Coverage Details

Benefit Amount Disability insurance policies usually replace a percentage of the policyholder's pre-disability income, commonly between 50% and 70%. The specific amount depends on the policy's terms and the premium paid.

Benefit Period The length of time benefits are paid varies by policy. Short-term policies may offer benefits for a few months, Long-term insurance, on the other hand, may pay out payments for as long as a lifetime, not just a few years.

Elimination Period The elimination period refers to the duration between the start of a disability and the commencement of benefits. Shorter elimination periods result in higher premiums, while more extended periods lower the premium cost.

Definitions of Disability Policies define disability in various ways, affecting eligibility for benefits. "Own occupation" insurance provides benefits if the insured is unable to do their own profession, while "any occupation" policies necessitate that the insured be unable to perform any employment. to carry out any task for which they possess the necessary qualifications.

Eligibility and Application

Applicants for disability insurance undergo underwriting, which assesses the individual's health, occupation, income, and lifestyle. This process determines eligibility, coverage details, and premium rates. Pre-existing conditions and high-risk occupations may affect coverage terms and costs.

Claims Process

Notification and Documentation To initiate a claim, the insured must notify the insurer promptly following a disabling event and provide comprehensive medical documentation supporting the disability claim.

Evaluation and Approval The insurer evaluates the claim against the policy's terms, which may involve a review by medical professionals and verification of employment and income. Once approved, the insurer calculates the benefit amount and begins payments.

Continuation of Benefits Beneficiaries may be required to provide ongoing proof of disability, such as regular medical updates, to continue receiving benefits. Insurers may also offer rehabilitation or job training services to assist in the return to work, if possible.

Challenges and Considerations

Navigating disability insurance requires understanding the intricate details of policy coverage, including the definitions of disability, benefit periods, and the impact of policy exclusions. Individuals should carefully assess their financial needs and risk exposure to choose the most appropriate type and level of coverage.

Disability insurance plays a vital role in ensuring financial security in the face of unforeseen health challenges. Providing a replacement income during periods of disability allows individuals and families to maintain their standard of living, manage medical and living expenses, and focus on recovery and rehabilitation. With careful planning and consideration of individual needs, disability insurance can be a cornerstone of a comprehensive financial strategy, safeguarding against the economic impact of disability.

Additional and Special Policies

In the realm of insurance, additional and special policies play a crucial role in providing comprehensive coverage that extends beyond the standard provisions of primary policies. These policies are designed to address specific risks, situations, or needs that may not be fully covered under traditional health, life, disability, or social insurance plans. This detailed note explores the variety of additional and special policies available, their importance, and how they complement existing coverage.

Understanding Additional and Special Policies

Purpose and Importance The primary aim of additional and special policies is to fill coverage gaps left by standard insurance policies. They offer targeted protection against particular risks, ensuring individuals and businesses can safeguard against unforeseen financial losses that could arise from specific events or circumstances.

Types of Additional and Special Policies

- **Critical Illness Insurance**: Provides a single payout after the verification of certain criteria, such as the occurrence of cancer, heart attack, or stroke. This insurance coverage aids in mitigating the exorbitant expenses linked to critical medical issues.
- **Long-term support Insurance** often covers long-term care services, for example nursing facility care, assisted living, or home care, that are generally not included in Medicare or basic health insurance.
- **Accidental Death and Dismemberment (AD&D) Insurance:** Provides compensation in the case of accidental death or specified injuries, such as the loss of a limb or vision. It functions as an adjunct to life insurance.
- **Travel Insurance:** Provides comprehensive coverage for a range of travel-related risks, such as trip cancellations, medical crises in foreign countries, lost baggage, and accidental death or injury while traveling.
- **Pet Insurance:** Covers veterinary expenses for pets, offering protection against the financial impact of medical care for illnesses or injuries.
- **Flood Insurance:** Provides coverage for damage to property due to flooding, which is typically excluded from standard homeowners' insurance policies.

Coverage Details and Considerations

Every supplementary and unique insurance has its own distinct coverage details, eligibility requirements, and limitations. Comprehending these particular details is essential for assessing the suitability of the coverage for the requirements of a person or a company.

Customization and Flexibility Many additional and special policies offer a high degree of customization, allowing policyholders to select coverage limits, deductibles, and specific provisions that best meet their needs. This flexibility ensures that the coverage closely aligns with the individual's risk exposure and financial situation.

Cost-Benefit Analysis When considering additional and special policies, it's essential to conduct a thorough cost-benefit analysis. This involves weighing the premium costs against the potential financial impact of not having coverage for specific risks. A careful assessment of personal or business risk factors and financial priorities should inform the decision to purchase such policies.

Complementing Existing Coverage

Additional and special policies should not be viewed in isolation but rather as part of a comprehensive insurance strategy. They complement existing coverage, providing an extra layer of financial protection and peace of mind. Policyholders should review their overall insurance portfolio regularly to identify any gaps that additional policies could fill.

Challenges and Decision-Making

Navigating the landscape of additional and special policies can be complex, given the vast array of options and detailed provisions involved. Consulting with insurance experts or financial consultants may assist individuals and organizations in making well-informed choices about the inclusion of policies in their insurance portfolios.

Additional and special policies offer vital protection against a broad spectrum of risks not typically covered by standard insurance policies. Whether it's guarding against the financial toll of a critical illness, ensuring care during old age, or protecting assets from natural disasters, these policies provide targeted coverage to meet specific needs. By carefully selecting additional and special policies, individuals and businesses can achieve a more comprehensive and tailored insurance strategy, ensuring robust protection against the diverse risks they face.

ADDITIONAL CONCEPTS

AND TRENDS

The insurance sector is in a constant state of transformation, propelled by technology progress, expanding customer demands, regulatory changes, and rising hazards. This dynamism introduces new concepts and trends that shape the future of insurance, offering both challenges and opportunities for insurers and policyholders alike. This chapter explores these developments, highlighting how they impact the insurance landscape and what they mean for the future.

Digital Transformation

Insurtech The rise of insurtech—startups and technology-driven innovations focused on enhancing or disrupting traditional insurance models—has been a game-changer. From AI-driven risk assessments and blockchain for fraud prevention to telematics in auto insurance and robo-advisors for personalized policy recommendations, insurtech is reshaping customer experiences and operational efficiencies.

Online Platforms and Mobile Apps Digital platforms and mobile apps have transformed the way consumers purchase and manage insurance. These tools offer increased convenience, enabling policy comparison, online purchasing, digital claims processing, and real-time customer support. As a result, insurers are investing in digital channels to meet the growing demand for tech-savvy solutions.

Personalized and Usage-Based Insurance (UBI)

Advancements in data analytics and IoT devices have paved the way for more personalized insurance products. Usage-based insurance models, especially in auto and health insurance, adjust premiums based on individual behavior, rewarding safe driving or healthy lifestyles. Similarly, big data enables insurers to tailor coverage and pricing to policyholders' unique risk profiles, enhancing value and fairness.

Cyber Insurance

As cyber threats become more prevalent, the demand for cyber insurance has surged. These policies cover a range of cyber risks, including data breaches, cyber-attacks, and system disruptions. Given the financial and reputational stakes, businesses and individuals alike are recognizing the importance of cyber insurance in their risk management strategies.

Climate Change and Sustainability

The impact of climate change has significant implications for the insurance industry, particularly in terms of natural disaster risk. Insurers are increasingly focusing on sustainability, both in underwriting practices and in investing insurance premiums. Furthermore, products that provide compensation based on specified triggers instead of the conventional claims procedure, such as parametric insurance and climate risk insurance, are becoming more popular.

Regulatory and Ethical Considerations

Data Privacy and Protection As insurers leverage personal data for underwriting and personalized pricing, issues of data protection and privacy come to the forefront. Regulatory frameworks like the GDPR in Europe and various state regulations in the US are shaping how insurers collect, use, and secure policyholder data.

Ethical AI The use of artificial intelligence in underwriting, claims processing, and customer service raises ethical concerns, particularly regarding bias and fairness. Insurers are tasked with ensuring that AI systems are explainable, transparent, and free from discriminatory biases.

The Gig Economy and New Employment Models

The rise of the gig economy and non-traditional employment models is challenging the traditional boundaries of workplace benefits, including insurance. Insurers are developing new products and services to cater to freelancers, gig workers, and entrepreneurs who require flexible and portable insurance solutions.

The insurance sector is at an inflection point, with new concepts and trends driving significant changes in how insurance products are designed, delivered, and consumed. As the industry navigates these developments, the focus remains on enhancing risk protection, improving customer experiences, and addressing emerging challenges. For insurers, staying ahead of these trends is crucial for competitive advantage. For policyholders, these changes promise more personalized, efficient, and responsive insurance solutions tailored to the complexities of modern life and work.

Market News and Trends

In the ever-evolving financial markets, staying abreast of the latest news and trends is crucial for investors, businesses, and policymakers alike. From geopolitical events and economic indicators to technological innovations and regulatory changes, numerous factors can influence market dynamics. This guide outlines key areas to watch in market news and trends, providing insights into their potential impacts.

Global Economic Indicators

Economic indicators are vital for understanding the health and direction of global economies. Key metrics include GDP growth rates, unemployment figures, inflation rates, and consumer confidence indexes. A rising GDP suggests economic expansion, while high unemployment may signal economic distress. Tracking these indicators across major economies can provide a comprehensive view of global economic trends.

Monetary Policy and Central Banks

Market trends are significantly shaped by central bank decisions, such as those made by the Federal Reserve in the United States, the European Central Bank (ECB), and the Bank of Japan (BOJ). Decisions on interest rates, quantitative easing initiatives, and monetary policy declarations may have a big impact on bond yields, currency values, and stock market performance. Investors keep a close eye on moves taken by central banks to determine the direction of economic policy and how it affects investing strategy.

Geopolitical Events and Trade Relations

Geopolitical events, including elections, trade negotiations, and conflicts, can create volatility in the markets. Trade relations between major economies, such as the US-China trade war or Brexit negotiations, have far-reaching implications for global trade dynamics, supply chains, and currency markets. Keeping an eye on these developments is essential for understanding their potential impact on investment portfolios and business operations.

Technological Innovations and Disruptions

Technological advancements are reshaping industries and market landscapes. Innovations in artificial intelligence, blockchain, renewable energy, and biotechnology present new investment opportunities and challenges. Disruptive technologies can redefine competitive landscapes, creating winners and losers across sectors. Investors and businesses must stay informed about technological trends to identify growth opportunities and mitigate risks.

Environmental, Social, and Governance (ESG) Investing

ESG investing has gained momentum, driven by increasing awareness of climate change, social justice, and corporate governance issues. Investors are allocating capital toward companies with strong ESG credentials, influencing corporate behaviors and market trends. Tracking the growth of ESG-focused funds and the performance of ESG benchmarks can provide insights into the sustainability trend's impact on markets.

Regulatory Changes and Implications

Regulatory environments across sectors are constantly evolving, with significant implications for businesses and investors. Changes in financial regulations, data protection laws, and environmental standards can affect company operations and market competitiveness. Staying informed about regulatory trends is crucial for compliance and strategic planning.

Market Sentiment and Investor Behavior

Market sentiment, influenced by news, economic data, and global events, can drive short-term market movements. Investor behavior, including the shift towards passive investing and the rise of retail investors participating through platforms like Robin hood, is reshaping market dynamics. Analyzing investor sentiment indicators and fund flow data can provide valuable insights into potential reversals and market trends.

The Rise of Digital Assets and Cryptocurrencies

The emergence of cryptocurrencies and digital assets represents a new frontier in financial markets. As these assets gain acceptance among investors and regulatory frameworks evolve, understanding the trends in the crypto market, including the adoption of blockchain technology by traditional financial institutions, is essential for a forward-looking investment strategy.

The complexity and interconnectivity of global markets demand a multifaceted approach to understanding news and trends. By focusing on economic indicators, monetary policy, geopolitical events, technological innovations, ESG investing, regulatory changes, market sentiment, and the rise of digital assets, stakeholders can navigate the markets more effectively. Keeping informed and analyzing these trends enables investors, businesses, and policymakers to make well-informed decisions, capitalize on opportunities, and mitigate risks in a rapidly changing world.

Implications for Agents and Brokers

The insurance sector is experiencing substantial changes due to technology progress, evolving customer demands, regulatory changes, and rising hazards. These changes present both challenges and opportunities for insurance agents and brokers, who play a crucial role in connecting clients with insurance products that meet their needs. Understanding the implications of industry trends for agents and brokers is essential for adapting strategies, enhancing service delivery, and ensuring sustained success in a competitive market.

Technology and Digitization

The Rise of Insurtech The proliferation of insurtech startups has introduced innovative technologies and business models to the insurance sector, challenging traditional practices. Agents and brokers must navigate this new landscape by embracing digital tools that enhance efficiency, improve client interactions, and offer competitive products.

Digital Platforms and Customer Expectations Consumers increasingly expect seamless, digital-first interactions. Agents and brokers must leverage online platforms, mobile apps, and digital communication channels to meet these expectations, providing convenient access to information, quotes, and customer service.

Big Data and Analytics Advanced analytics and big data offer agents and brokers insights into customer behavior, risk profiles, and market trends. Utilizing these tools can enable more personalized service, targeted marketing strategies, and informed risk assessment.

Regulatory and Compliance Changes

The insurance industry is subject to evolving regulatory standards aimed at protecting consumer interests and promoting market stability. Agents and brokers must stay informed about regulatory changes in their regions, ensuring compliance and guiding clients through the complexities of the insurance landscape.

The Shift toward Personalization

As insurers develop more personalized products, agents and brokers have the opportunity to offer tailored insurance solutions. Understanding individual client needs, leveraging data-driven insights, and maintaining a deep knowledge of available products are essential for personalizing service and enhancing client satisfaction.

The Growing Importance of Cyber Insurance

With cyber threats on the rise, there is increasing demand for cyber insurance products. Agents and brokers who specialize in this area or develop expertise in cyber risk management can position themselves as valuable advisors to clients navigating digital vulnerabilities.

Sustainability and ESG Considerations

The consideration of environmental, social, and governance (ESG) aspects is becoming more crucial when purchasing insurance. Agents and brokers can differentiate themselves by understanding ESG trends, advising clients on sustainable insurance products, and incorporating ESG considerations into their business practices.

New Risks and Emerging Markets

The emergence of new risks, such as those associated with climate change, pandemics, and technological disruption, requires agents and brokers to update their knowledge and continuously adapt their offerings. Staying ahead of trends and emerging risks enables agents and brokers to advise clients proactively and secure coverage that addresses evolving needs.

The Role of Education and Advisory Services

As products and the risk landscape become more complex, clients rely more heavily on agents and brokers for guidance. Offering educational resources and advisory services can strengthen client relationships, build trust, and position agents and brokers as trusted advisors.

The role of agents and brokers is evolving in response to industry trends, technological advancements, and changing client expectations. By embracing innovation, adapting to regulatory changes, leveraging data, and focusing on personalization and advisory services, agents and brokers can navigate the challenges and capitalize on the opportunities presented by the dynamic insurance landscape. Success in this new era requires a commitment to continuous learning, flexibility, and a client-centric approach, ensuring agents and brokers remain indispensable partners in risk management.

QUESTIONS AND ANSWERS

As we delve into the complex world of life and health insurance, understanding the nuances of various policies and their implications is crucial for both aspiring professionals preparing for their exams and individuals navigating their insurance options. The Q&A section of this book aims to distill complex information into accessible insights, providing clear and comprehensive answers to some of the most pertinent questions in the field. Through this approach, we endeavor to equip readers with the knowledge and understanding necessary to make informed decisions, whether they're studying for certification or seeking the best insurance coverage to meet their needs.

Q: What distinguishes term life insurance from permanent life insurance?
A: As the name implies, term life insurance covers a certain time frame, or "term," and in the event of the insured's death, the policy pays out a death benefit. The opposite is true with permanent life insurance, which offers continuous coverage during a person's whole life along with a death benefit. Furthermore, it often includes a component of monetary worth that grows progressively over the course of time.

Q: How does whole life insurance accumulate cash value?
A: Whole life insurance builds up cash value by allocating a part of the premiums paid by the insured. The insurer allocates this money for investment purposes and the cash value increases without being subject to immediate taxation for the duration of the insurance.

Q: Can you convert a term life insurance policy into a permanent one?
A: Actually, policyholders may turn their term life insurance into a permanent policy with certain plans' conversion options, and it doesn't even need a new medical exam! This conversion often occurs before the expiration of the term policy or when the policyholder attains a certain age.

Q: What is universal life insurance, and how is it flexible?
A: A kind of permanent life insurance with adjustable premiums and death payouts is called universal life insurance. In accordance with their evolving financial demands, policyholders may modify the amount of their death benefit and premium payments, subject to certain restrictions.

Q: How do variable life insurance policies differ from other permanent policies?
A: The cash value of a variable life insurance policy may be invested in a number of ways, the most common of which are mutual funds, equities, and bonds. The death benefit and cash value might rise and fall depending on how well these assets do, exposing you to more risk but also increasing the possibility of greater gain.

Q: What is a survivorship life insurance policy?
A: Survivorship life insurance, also known as second-to-die insurance, provides coverage for two persons, usually couples, and only pays the death benefit after both insured individuals have died. It is often used for the purpose of estate planning.

Q: How does a decreasing term life insurance policy work?
A: A decreasing term life insurance policy features a death benefit that diminishes over time, usually in line with a decreasing liability, such as a mortgage. Premiums generally remain level while the coverage amount decreases.

Q: What role does the cash value in a whole life policy play in borrowing or withdrawals?
A: The cash value inside a whole-life insurance policy might serve as collateral for obtaining a loan from the insurance company or for making withdrawals. Loans must be repaid with interest to avoid reducing the death benefit, while withdrawals decrease the cash value and potentially the death benefit.

Q: Explain the tax implications of the cash value component in permanent life insurance policies.
A: Permanent life insurance plans have cash values that increase tax-deferred, delaying payment of taxes on interest or capital gains until the money is withdrawn. Furthermore, the death benefit may be transferred to recipients tax-free if handled appropriately.

Q: What is the return of a premium term life insurance policy?
A: If the insured lives out the policy term, a return of premium term life insurance policy reimburses the premiums paid. Because of the additional advantage of the premium return, these plans are more costly than typical term insurance.

Q: Can you increase the death benefit in a universal life insurance policy?
A: Yes, policyholders can often increase the death benefit in a universal life insurance policy, subject to insurability and underwriting approval. This allows for flexibility to adjust coverage as financial needs change.

Q: What is the primary benefit of a level-term life insurance policy?
A: The primary benefit of a level-term life insurance policy is that it provides a fixed death benefit and premium payments that do not change throughout the term, making budgeting easier for policyholders.

Q: How might inflation affect the purchasing power of a fixed death benefit from a life insurance policy?
A: Inflation can erode the purchasing power of a fixed death benefit over time, meaning the amount may not cover as much in terms of expenses or financial needs in the future as it does when the policy is first issued.

Q: Why might someone choose a joint life insurance policy?
A: Someone might choose a joint life insurance policy to cover two lives under one policy, often for married couples. This type of policy can be cost-effective and valuable for estate planning or providing for dependents after both policyholders have passed.

Q: How does the cost of insurance charges affect a universal life insurance policy?

A: A universal life insurance policy's cash value decreases due to the cost of insurance (COI) costs, which cover various expenditures and the risk of death. If the policyholder's premiums are not adequate to cover the COI, the policy may expire or they may need to be paid in extra installments.

Q: What does the incontestability clause in an insurance policy signify?

A: The incontestability clause protects the policyholder by limiting the insurer's ability to contest the validity of the insurance contract after it has been in force for a specific period, typically two years, except in cases of fraud.

Q: How does a waiver of premium rider benefit the policyholder in times of hardship?
A: This rider ensures that the insurance remains active without any additional financial strain throughout the disability term by exempting the policyholder from paying premiums in the event of complete disability.

Q: Can you explain the function of an accidental death benefit rider?
A: In the case that the insured person's demise is a result of an accident, this rider provides an additional death payment, which often doubles the base policy value. The recipients are therefore provided with a higher level of financial stability.

Q: What is the purpose of the guaranteed insurability option in a life insurance policy?
A: The policyholder is given the opportunity to buy more insurance at certain future dates without needing a medical exam or proof of insurability. This protects against the possibility of becoming uninsurable because of changes in health.

Q: How do policy exclusions for pre-existing conditions affect coverage?

A: These exclusions prevent the policy from paying out for claims related to health issues that the insured had prior to the policy's effective date, thereby limiting the insurer's risk.

Q: What is a conversion option in term life insurance, and why is it valuable?
A: By enabling policyholders to convert their term life policies into permanent ones without a medical evaluation, the conversion option ensures that insurance coverage remains available in the event of future health changes.

Q: How does a long-term care rider enhance a life insurance policy?

A: This rider provides financial benefits to cover long-term care services, such as nursing home or in-home care, which are not typically covered under standard health or disability insurance.

Q: What implications do loan provisions in a life insurance policy have for the policy's cash value and death benefit?
A: If the loan taken against the cash value of the policy is not returned, it might result in a reduction of the death benefit. This reduction occurs because the loan amount, together with the interest, is subtracted from the amount given to the beneficiaries.

Q: How do cost of living adjustment riders in disability insurance policies benefit the insured?

A: These riders adjust the benefit amount annually based on inflation rates, ensuring that the disability payments maintain their purchasing power over time.

Q: What is the impact of a policy's suicide exclusion?
A: In order to reduce the insurer's risk, If the policyholder intentionally takes their own life within a certain period, typically two years after the commencement of the policy, the claim for the death benefit will be denied.

Q: How does the return of premium option in term insurance work?

A: It refunds the premiums paid if the insured survives the term period, effectively providing coverage at no net cost if the benefit is not used.

Q: What are the benefits and limitations of adding a critical illness rider to a health insurance policy?

A: Benefits include receiving a lump-sum payment upon diagnosis of a covered illness and aiding with expenses not covered by traditional health insurance. Limitations might consist of specific definitions of covered illnesses and waiting periods.

Q: How does the automatic premium loan provision protect the policyholder?

A: It automatically applies a loan against the cash value to pay premiums if the policyholder fails to do so, preventing the policy from lapsing due to non-payment.

Q: What does an exclusion for dangerous activities entail in an insurance policy?

A: This exclusion denies coverage for claims resulting from engagement in high-risk activities specified in the policy, such as skydiving or motor racing.

Q: How does a reinstatement provision benefit a policyholder whose coverage has lapsed?

A: It allows the policyholder to reinstate lapsed coverage under certain conditions, typically involving evidence of insurability and payment of back premiums, maintaining the original policy benefits without starting anew.

Q: What role does the grace period provision play in maintaining insurance coverage?

A: The grace period provision in an insurance policy is designed to protect policyholders from immediate policy cancellation due to a missed premium payment. Typically spanning 30 days, this provision allows policyholders extra time to make their payment and keep their coverage active, ensuring that a brief financial hiccup doesn't lead to a loss of vital insurance protection.

Q: How does an underwriting period impact the issuance of an insurance policy?

A: The underwriting period is a critical phase in the policy issuance process where the insurer assesses the risk of insuring the applicant based on their health, lifestyle, and financial status. This evaluation can affect premium rates, coverage limits, and even the decision to offer coverage. A thorough and accurate underwriting process ensures that the policy terms are fair and reflective of the risk the insurer is taking on, ultimately impacting the policyholder's costs and coverage benefits.

Q: Describe the benefits of a child term rider added to a life insurance policy.
A: A kid-term rider gives the policyholder's children short-term life insurance coverage and pays a death payment in the event that a child dies before a certain age. This rider is particularly beneficial as it spares parents the financial burden of funeral and burial expenses during an already emotionally devastating time. Furthermore, it often permits conversion to a permanent policy without requiring proof of insurability, guaranteeing the child's ability to get insurance in the future.

Q: Explain the significance of the renewable term insurance provision.
A: Renewable term insurance allows the policyholder to extend their term policy for further durations without requiring a fresh medical examination, regardless of any deterioration in their health. This provision is significant as it ensures continued coverage despite changes in health status, providing peace of mind to policyholders that their insurance protection will not lapse just when they might need it most.

Q: How do exclusions for specific medical conditions affect health insurance coverage?

A: Exclusions for specific medical conditions in a health insurance policy mean that costs related to those conditions are not covered, shifting the financial burden of treatment onto the policyholder. This can significantly impact individuals with chronic illnesses or pre-existing conditions by increasing their out-of-pocket healthcare expenses, underscoring the importance of carefully reviewing policy exclusions before purchasing.

Q: What is the purpose of a cost of living adjustment (COLA) rider in disability insurance?

A: A COLA rider in a disability insurance policy adjusts the benefit amount based on inflation rates, ensuring that the purchasing power of disability benefits remains consistent over time. This is especially critical for long-term disabilities, where the cost of living is likely to increase, potentially diminishing the value of fixed benefits. The COLA rider protects against this risk, providing financial security to the disabled policyholder.

Q: How does a guaranteed renewability feature benefit the insured in health insurance policies?

A: Guaranteed renewability ensures that the policyholder can renew their health insurance policy every year without facing cancellation or significant changes in terms by the insurer, regardless of any changes in health status. This feature is beneficial as it offers stability and long-term security to the insured, knowing that their health coverage will continue as needed without unexpected interruptions or conditions.

Q: Describe the implications of a pre-existing condition waiting period in health insurance.

A: A pre-existing condition waiting period in health insurance is a designated period during which claims related to conditions the insured had before obtaining the new policy are not covered. This can delay necessary treatments and impose financial burdens on individuals, highlighting the importance of understanding policy terms and considering coverage options carefully, especially for those with ongoing health issues.

Q: What does an accidental death and dismemberment (AD&D) rider entail?
A: Additional benefits are provided to the beneficiary by an AD&D rider in the event of an dismemberment, such as the loss of limbs or sight, to the insured or accidental death. This rider supplements the base policy benefit, often doubling the payout in the event of an accidental death, which can be instrumental in covering unforeseen financial needs or maintaining the family's standard of living after such a tragic event.

Q: Explain the impact of lifetime maximum benefits in health insurance policies.

A: Lifetime maximum benefits refer to the total amount an insurance policy will pay out over the lifetime of the insured. Once this limit is reached, the policyholder must cover all subsequent medical expenses out of pocket. This can pose significant financial risks for individuals with chronic illnesses or long-term healthcare needs, emphasizing the importance of selecting policies with adequate coverage limits to ensure comprehensive protection.

Q: How do non-forfeiture options benefit a life insurance policyholder?**
A: A life insurance policy's non-forfeiture options safeguard the policyholder's rights in the event that they are unable to make premium payments. With options like cash surrender value, extended term insurance, or decreased paid-up insurance, the policyholder may still take advantage of the policy's value without having to pay more premiums. This ensures that the policyholder does not entirely lose their investment in the policy due to financial difficulties, providing a safety net that can adapt to changing economic circumstances.

Q: What considerations should be made when selecting a long-term care rider on a life insurance policy?

A: When selecting a long-term care rider, considerations should include the rider's cost versus standalone long-term care insurance, the types of care covered (e.g., in-home care, assisted living), benefit triggers, and the potential impact on the life insurance death benefit. This rider can significantly extend the utility of a life insurance policy, but it's essential to weigh its benefits against individual health risk factors and financial planning goals to ensure it aligns with broader insurance needs.

Q: How does the portability feature in health insurance policies affect policyholders?

A: Portability allows policyholders to maintain their health insurance coverage without losing benefits when changing jobs or experiencing other life transitions. This feature is crucial in ensuring continuous health coverage, especially for those with pre-existing conditions or ongoing healthcare needs, by eliminating gaps in coverage that could lead to financial vulnerability due to uncovered medical expenses.

Q: Describe the benefit of adding an inflation protection rider to a long-term care insurance policy.

A: An inflation protection rider on a long-term care insurance policy adjusts the benefit amount to keep pace with inflation, ensuring that the policy's benefits will be sufficient to cover future long-term care costs. Given the rising cost of healthcare services, this rider is essential for maintaining the purchasing power of the benefits, safeguarding against the risk that inflation will erode the policy's effectiveness over time.

Q: What are the financial implications of a policy's suicide exclusion clause for beneficiaries?
A: A suicide exclusion clause often states that the insurance company will not deliver the death benefit if the insured individual takes their own life during a certain period after the policy's commencement, typically two years. Financially, this means beneficiaries may only receive a refund of the premiums paid rather than the full death benefit, placing significant importance on understanding all policy terms and conditions to prevent unforeseen financial consequences for the insured's loved ones.

How does life insurance fit into a retirement planning strategy?

A: Life insurance can play a pivotal role in retirement planning by providing a death benefit that secures financial stability for dependents, offering cash value components in permanent policies that can supplement retirement income, and serving as a tool for estate planning to ensure wealth is transferred according to the policyholder's wishes. It's a versatile tool that can protect against the risk of premature death while also offering potential cash value growth.

Q: What are the tax implications of withdrawing cash value from a life insurance policy?
A: Withdrawals from the cash value of a life insurance policy are exempt from taxes as long as they do not exceed the amount of premiums paid. Any sum that is taken in excess of the premiums paid is subject to taxation as regular income. Policyholders should thoroughly evaluate the tax implications and seek guidance from a tax expert prior to making withdrawals in order to prevent unforeseen tax obligations.

Q: How do annuities complement life insurance in financial planning?

A: Annuities and life insurance complement each other by addressing different financial needs: annuities provide guaranteed income during retirement, ensuring the policyholder won't outlive their assets, while life insurance offers financial protection to beneficiaries upon the policyholder's death. Together, they can provide a comprehensive approach to financial security, covering both longevity risk and the need for legacy planning.

Q: Can life insurance proceeds be subject to estate taxes?
A: The life insurance payout might be subject to inheritance taxes if the policyholder is considered the owner after death and their estate is larger than the exemption amounts set by the federal government or individual states. Nevertheless, using effective estate planning strategies, such as establishing ownership of the policy via an irrevocable life insurance trust (ILIT), may effectively reduce or eliminate estate taxes on the death benefit.

Q: What role does a life insurance trust play in estate planning?

A: A life insurance trust, specifically an irrevocable life insurance trust (ILIT), holds a life insurance policy outside the insured's estate, allowing the death benefit to bypass the estate and directly benefit the trust's beneficiaries. This setup can protect the proceeds from estate taxes and creditors, providing more control over the distribution of assets and ensuring that the death benefit is used according to the grantor's wishes.

Q: How can business owners use life insurance for succession planning?
A: Entrepreneurs may use life insurance as a crucial instrument in succession planning by implementing buy-sell agreements that are financed by life insurance policies. Upon the death of a business owner, the policy proceeds can be used to buy out the deceased owner's interest, providing liquidity to the business and ensuring a smooth transition of ownership without financial strain.

Q: What is the Pension Maximization strategy involving life insurance?

A: Pension Maximization is a strategy where an individual nearing retirement opts for a higher pension payout option (single-life annuity) and uses some of the extra income to purchase a life insurance policy. This approach aims to maximize pension income while the policyholder is alive, with the life insurance benefit providing for their spouse after their death. It offers a more favorable financial outcome than choosing a joint survivor pension option.

Q: Are there any age limits for purchasing life insurance?

A: While there's no universal age limit for purchasing life insurance, options and costs can vary significantly with age. Older applicants may face higher premiums and limited policy options, particularly for term life insurance. Permanent policies may be more accessible but still come with higher costs due to increased risk. Insurers set their own age limits and underwriting criteria, making it essential to shop around and understand the specific policies of different insurers.

Q: How does the Modified Endowment Contract (MEC) status affect life insurance policies?

A: A life insurance policy can be classified as a Modified Endowment Contract (MEC) if it fails the IRS's 7-Pay Test, essentially meaning too much premium is paid into the policy too quickly. MECs lose the favorable tax treatment of loans and withdrawals, which become taxable to the extent of the policy's gains and may also be subject to a 10% penalty if taken before age 59½. This status highlights the importance of structuring premium payments carefully to avoid adverse tax consequences.

Q: What is critical person insurance, and how does it benefit a business?
A: An organization may choose to purchase a life insurance policy for a crucial employee whose departure would significantly impact the company's operations and financial stability. This kind of coverage is known as key person insurance. . The business is the beneficiary and uses the death benefit to mitigate economic losses, recruit a replacement, or cover debts. This insurance is crucial for the continuity and stability of the business.

Q: How can life insurance support retirement planning?

A: Life insurance can play a vital role in retirement planning by providing a death benefit that can support surviving family members or by accumulating a cash value that can be used as a tax-advantaged savings vehicle. Specific permanent life insurance policies allow policyholders to withdraw or borrow against the cash value, offering a supplementary source of retirement income.

Q: What are the tax implications of withdrawing from the cash value of a life insurance policy?
A: Withdrawals from the cash value of a life insurance policy are tax-exempt, provided that they do not surpass the entire sum of premiums paid. Nevertheless, any withdrawals above the whole amount of premiums paid are liable to income tax. Policy loans are generally not taxable, provided the policy is not classified as a Modified Endowment Contract (MEC).

Q: Can life insurance proceeds be subject to estate taxes?
A: Indeed, if the insured is deemed the owner of the policy at the time of their demise or if the benefits are receivable to their estate, the life insurance profits may be liable to estate taxes. Implementing effective estate planning strategies, such as establishing an irrevocable life insurance trust (ILIT), may mitigate the financial burden of inheritance taxes on life insurance benefits.

Q: How does a life insurance policy's beneficiary designation impact the payout process?

A: The beneficiary designation directly impacts the payout process, as it dictates who receives the death benefit upon the insured's passing. Clearly naming and regularly updating beneficiaries ensures that the death benefit is distributed according to the policyholder's wishes, potentially bypassing probate.

Q: What is a Modified Endowment Contract (MEC), and why is it significant for policyholders?

A: A Modified Endowment Contract (MEC) is a life insurance policy that fails the IRS's 7-pay Test, essentially classifying policies that are overfunded according to IRS limits. Withdrawals or loans from an MEC are taxed on a last-in-first-out (LIFO) basis, and premature distributions may incur a 10% penalty, making it significant for tax planning.

Q: How do annuity riders in life insurance policies benefit retirees?

A: Annuity riders can convert a portion of the life insurance death benefit into a stream of income for the policyholder, offering a financial planning tool for retirees seeking predictable income. This can provide additional retirement income while still leaving a portion of the death benefit intact for beneficiaries.

Q: What is the role of a contingent beneficiary in a life insurance policy?

A: A contingent beneficiary is the party designated to receive the death benefit if the primary beneficiary is unable to do so, typically due to predeceasing the insured or failing to meet other conditions. Naming a contingent beneficiary ensures that the death benefit is distributed according to the policyholder's intentions, even if circumstances change.

Q: How can a buy-sell agreement funded by life insurance benefit a business partnership?
A: A life insurance-funded buy-sell agreement establishes a method for the surviving partners to purchase the ownership stake of a dead partner, ensuring business continuity and preventing conflicts among survivors. The death benefit is used to purchase the deceased partner's share from their estate, offering a clear transition plan.

Q: What considerations should policyholders make regarding life insurance and charitable giving?

A: Policyholders can name a charity as a beneficiary of their life insurance policy, providing a significant gift that may exceed what could have been donated in cash during the policyholder's lifetime. This approach offers potential estate tax benefits and ensures a lasting legacy, but policyholders should consider the impact on family beneficiaries and consult financial advisors to maximize tax advantages.

Q: How does a return of premium features work in term life insurance?
A: In the event that the policyholder passes away while the policy is in force, the premiums paid may be refunded in whole or in part according to the return of premium provision in term life insurance. This feature increases the policy's cost but can be attractive for those seeking the security of term insurance with the possibility of getting their premiums back.

Q: Why might a policyholder consider a life settlement option?

A: A policyholder might consider a life settlement, selling their life insurance policy to a third party for a lump sum that is less than the death benefit but more than the cash surrender value if they no longer need the coverage, find the premiums unaffordable, or wish to access the policy's value for other needs. This option provides financial flexibility but requires careful consideration of the long-term implications.

Q: How do HMO plans manage patient care?
A: HMO (Health Maintenance Organization) plans to manage patient care through a network of providers. Patients choose a primary care physician (PCP) who organizes all their healthcare services, including sending them to specialists inside the network, to guarantee coordinated and cost-efficient treatment.

Q: What distinguishes PPO plans from HMOs?

A: PPO (Preferred Provider Organization) plans to offer more flexibility than HMOs by allowing patients to see specialists and out-of-network providers without a referral, though at a higher cost. PPOs provide a balance between organized care and freedom of choice.

Q: Describe the unique features of EPO health insurance plans.
A: The Exclusive Provider Organization (EPO) intends to integrate PPO and HMO components. Similar to HMOs, they have a provider network and only pay for in-network treatment in an emergency. However, like PPOs, they don't require referrals to see specialists within the network.

Q: How do HDHPs encourage consumer-driven healthcare?

A: HDHPs (High Deductible Health Plans) have lower premiums and higher deductibles, encouraging individuals to be more conscious of healthcare spending. They're often paired with Health Savings Accounts (HSAs), allowing patients to use pre-tax dollars for medical expenses, fostering a consumer-driven approach to healthcare.

Q: What role do HSAs play in conjunction with HDHPs?
A: In addition to HDHPs, health savings accounts (HSAs) empower people to set aside money before taxes and use it to cover certain medical costs. HSAs help offset the higher deductibles of HDHPs, making healthcare costs more manageable while providing tax advantages.

Q: Can you explain the benefits of adding a critical illness rider to a health insurance policy?
A: A critical illness rider pays out a lump sum payout in the event that the policyholder is identified as having one of the designated critical diseases, such as cancer or heart disease. This may assist in deducting missed wages, out-of-pocket medical bills, and other costs not covered by typical health insurance.

Q: What are the advantages of group health insurance plans for employees?

A: Because most businesses contribute to the premiums for their employees' group health insurance policies, workers may usually get these plans at a reduced rate. They also provide the benefit of not requiring individual underwriting, making coverage more accessible to employees regardless of their health status.

Q: How does COBRA coverage work for individuals who lose their job?
A: For a certain time, usually up to 18 months, COBRA (Consolidated Omnibus Budget Reconciliation Act) allows people to maintain their employer-sponsored health insurance in the event that they lose their employment or have their hours reduced. But the person is responsible for paying the whole premium cost.

Q: What is the significance of the Affordable Care Act (ACA) in individual health insurance?
A: The ACA greatly increased the availability of individual health insurance by creating health insurance marketplaces, providing financial assistance to low-income individuals, and passing laws that make it illegal for insurance companies to discriminate against people because of their health status or refuse to cover those with pre-existing diseases.

Q: Describe how POS plans offer a blend of HMO and PPO features.
A: Like HMOs, POS (Point of Service) plans to demand the selection of a primary care physician, but they also provide members the option to visit out-of-network physicians for a premium, similar to PPOs. They provide a middle ground, offering structured care with more provider options.

Q: How do short-term health insurance plans differ from standard health policies?
A: Pre-existing condition exclusions and less comprehensive coverage are common features of short-term health insurance policies, which provide temporary coverage with restricted benefits. They are not a replacement for long-term health insurance options; rather, they are meant to fill insurance gaps, such as those resulting from changing employment.

Q: What are the potential benefits and drawbacks of a fixed indemnity health plan?

A: Fixed indemnity health plans pay a set cash benefit for specific medical services, regardless of the actual costs. While they can provide supplemental coverage to help with out-of-pocket expenses, they may only partially cover some medical costs, leaving gaps in coverage.

Q: How do catastrophic health insurance plans function?
A: Catastrophic health insurance plans are designed for young, healthy individuals. They offer protection against very high medical costs from serious accidents or illnesses. Their premiums are affordable, but their deductibles are very high. These plans mainly provide coverage for critical health benefits after the deductible has been paid. These plans are economically advantageous for those who need fundamental coverage and have the financial means to personally bear the expenses of regular healthcare treatments.

Q: Explain the importance of network size and quality in selecting a health insurance plan.

A: The size and quality of a health insurance plan's provider network are crucial because they determine the quality and accessibility of healthcare services available to policyholders. A more extensive network offers more choices for doctors and specialists, while a network with high-quality providers ensures better healthcare outcomes. Policyholders should consider both factors to make sure they have access to the best possible care within their plan's coverage terms.

Q: What considerations should individuals make regarding out-of-pocket maximums when choosing a health insurance plan?
A: Out-of-pocket maximums refer to the whole sum that a policyholder must spend for healthcare services covered by their policy during a year, excluding premiums. Choosing a plan with a lower out-of-pocket maximum can significantly reduce financial risk in case of significant health issues but may come with higher monthly premiums. Individuals should balance these costs with their economic situation and health needs to select the most appropriate plan.

Q: How does the Mental Health Parity Act affect health insurance coverage?
A: Under the Mental Health Parity Act, medical and surgical treatments must be covered at the same level as mental health and drug addiction treatment services by health insurance companies. This means limitations on benefits, copayments, and treatment approvals for mental health services cannot be more restrictive than those for physical health services, ensuring comprehensive coverage for mental health needs.

Q: Discuss the impact of telehealth services on health insurance coverage and healthcare access.
A: Patients may now get more healthcare services, including remote medical consultations, thanks to telehealth programs. Telehealth is becoming more widely covered by health insurance, which is convenient and eliminates the need for in-person consultations. This can lead to cost savings for both insurers and policyholders while increasing access to care, especially in rural or underserved areas.

Q: How do wellness programs integrated into health insurance policies benefit policyholders?

A: Wellness programs encourage policyholders to maintain a healthy lifestyle through incentives like premium discounts, gym memberships, or cash rewards for completing health assessments and participating in fitness activities. These programs can improve policyholders' health, potentially reducing healthcare costs and premiums over time by decreasing the need for medical services.

Q: What role do preventive care benefits play in health insurance plans?

A: Preventive care benefits cover services like vaccinations, screenings, and annual check-ups aimed at preventing illnesses or detecting health issues early when they are more treatable. These advantages have the potential to reduce healthcare expenses while improving policyholders' health in the long run by reducing the incidence of severe medical conditions that require expensive treatments.

Q: Explain the challenges and considerations of insuring individuals with pre-existing conditions before and after the ACA.

A: People who already had health issues often had to deal with increased rates, less coverage, or even outright rejection of insurance before the ACA. The ACA prohibited such practices, requiring plans to cover all applicants regardless of health status and to provide comprehensive coverage for pre-existing conditions. While this has increased access to insurance, it has also led to discussions about the sustainability of premiums and the balance of risk pools, highlighting the ongoing challenge of providing affordable, comprehensive health insurance to all individuals, regardless of their health history.

Q: How do mental health coverage provisions in health insurance policies impact treatment options for policyholders?

A: Mental health coverage provisions ensure policyholders have access to psychiatric care, counseling, and substance abuse treatment, similar to physical health treatments. This parity in coverage helps remove financial barriers to seeking mental health services, offering a broader range of treatment options and supporting overall well-being.

Q: What is the impact of a pre-existing condition exclusion period in a health insurance policy?

A: A pre-existing condition exclusion period temporarily restricts coverage for conditions that the policyholder had before enrolling in a new health plan. This can delay necessary treatment for those conditions, emphasizing the importance of understanding policy terms and considering coverage options carefully, especially for individuals with ongoing health issues.

Q: How does a no-claims bonus option work in health insurance policies?

A: A no-claims bonus in health insurance rewards policyholders with a discount or increased benefits for not filing any claims during a policy year. This option encourages healthy lifestyles and prudent use of insurance, potentially lowering premiums or enhancing coverage over time without additional cost.

Q: Explain how the coordination of benefits provision works when a policyholder has multiple health insurance policies.

A: The coordination of benefits provision determines how multiple health insurance policies share the cost of claims, designating one as primary and the other as secondary. This prevents double dipping, ensuring claims are paid efficiently and policyholders receive the benefits they're entitled to without exceeding the total cost of the covered services.

Q: What benefits does a maternity coverage rider offer in a health insurance policy?

A: A maternity coverage rider provides additional benefits for pregnancy, childbirth, and newborn care. This can include coverage for prenatal visits, delivery costs, and postnatal care, helping to reduce the out-of-pocket expenses associated with pregnancy and ensuring comprehensive care for mother and baby.

Q: How do lifetime maximum benefits in health insurance policies affect long-term coverage?

A: Lifetime maximum benefits cap the total amount a health insurance policy will pay over the policyholder's lifetime. Once this limit is reached, the policyholder must cover all subsequent medical expenses, potentially impacting long-term coverage, especially for individuals with chronic conditions or long-term healthcare needs.

Q: Describe the advantages and limitations of adding an international coverage rider to a health insurance policy.

A: An international coverage rider extends health insurance benefits to include medical care received outside the policyholder's home country, offering protection during travel or extended stays abroad. While it provides valuable coverage for emergencies or necessary treatments, it may come with higher premiums and exclusions for routine care or specific regions.

Q: What role does a prescription drug coverage option play in a health insurance policy?

A: Prescription drug coverage helps offset the cost of medications, covering a portion of the price for generic and brand-name drugs. This is crucial for managing chronic conditions and ensuring access to necessary treatments, but policyholders should be aware of formulary lists, copayments, and coverage limits.

Q: How does a wellness program rider benefit health insurance policyholders?

A: A wellness program rider offers incentives for policyholders to engage in healthy behaviors, such as discounts for gym memberships, free health screenings, or rewards for completing health assessments. These programs encourage proactive health management and can lead to lower healthcare costs over time.

Q: What implications do network restrictions have on policyholder's choice of healthcare providers?

A: Network restrictions limit the choice of healthcare providers to those within the insurer's network, potentially impacting the policyholder's ability to see their preferred doctors or specialists. Out-of-network services often result in higher out-of-pocket costs, emphasizing the need to carefully select a plan based on provider preferences and geographical coverage.

Q: Describe the process and importance of appealing a denied health insurance claim.

A: Appealing a denied health insurance claim involves submitting documentation and evidence to contest the insurer's decision. This process is crucial for policyholders to overturn unjust denials and receive rightful benefits potentially. Understanding the appeals process and policy provisions is critical to effectively challenging denials and securing coverage for necessary treatments.

Q: How do policy exclusions for experimental treatments affect access to innovative therapies?

A: Policy exclusions for experimental treatments limit coverage for unproven or investigational procedures and medications. While intended to mitigate financial risk for insurers, these exclusions can restrict policyholders' access to potentially life-saving innovative therapies not yet widely accepted or approved by regulatory bodies. Individuals seeking access to cutting-edge treatments may need to explore clinical trials or seek alternative funding sources, stressing the significance of knowing what is and isn't covered by health insurance and the possible need for additional insurance policies that provide more possibilities for experimental treatments.

Q: What does a telemedicine option in a health insurance policy entail, and how does it benefit policyholders?

A: A telemedicine option provides policyholders access to healthcare services via phone or the Internet, facilitating virtual consultations with medical professionals. This feature is particularly beneficial for its convenience, offering timely medical advice, reducing the need for in-person visits, and potentially lowering healthcare costs. It's precious for managing minor health issues or for follow-up consultations.

Q: How can a policy's emergency care provision impact out-of-pocket expenses during a medical emergency?

A: An emergency care provision outlines coverage for services received during a medical emergency, including ambulance services and emergency room visits. Understanding this provision is crucial as it dictates the policyholder's financial responsibility in such situations. Policies with broad emergency care coverage can significantly reduce out-of-pocket expenses, whereas more restrictive policies may leave the policyholder facing high costs for emergency treatments, especially if received out-of-network.

Q: Explain the significance of a policy's waiting period before certain benefits become available.

A: A waiting period in a health insurance policy is a designated time frame during which specific benefits are not yet available to the policyholder. This is common for benefits like dental care, vision services, or pre-existing conditions. The waiting period helps insurers mitigate risk by ensuring that the policy is in place for a certain amount of time before covering potentially high-cost services. For policyholders, understanding and planning for these waiting periods is essential to avoid unexpected gaps in coverage.

Q: How do exclusions for pre-existing conditions influence an individual's coverage and treatment options?

A: Exclusions for pre-existing conditions can significantly influence a policyholder's coverage by denying benefits for treatments related to health issues that existed prior to effective date of policy. This can lead to considerable out-of-pocket expenses for necessary care. While the ACA has limited such exclusions in significant medical policies, they may still apply to certain types of health insurance, underscoring the importance of thoroughly reviewing a policy's terms and considering supplemental coverage or alternative insurance options.

Q: What factors should policyholders consider when deciding between individual vs. family coverage options in health insurance policies?

A: When choosing between individual and family coverage options, policyholders should consider their family's overall health needs, the potential for adding dependents, and the financial implications of each option. Family coverage can offer a more cost-effective solution for covering multiple family members under one policy but may come with higher premiums than individual plans. Assessing the benefits, coverage limits, and cost-sharing requirements of each option can help policyholders make an informed decision that best fits their family's healthcare budget and needs.

Q: Describe the impact of annual coverage limits on a policyholder's healthcare expenses.

A: Annual coverage limitations restrict the maximum amount that an insurance policy may reimburse for eligible healthcare services within a single policy year. Once the maximum limit is reached, the policyholder becomes liable for any additional medical expenditures until the start of the following policy year. This can significantly impact a policyholder's healthcare expenses, especially for those requiring extensive medical care or expensive treatments, underscoring the need to select a policy with adequate annual limits to cover anticipated healthcare needs.

Q: How does a health insurance policy's outpatient coverage provision affect access to day surgeries and procedures?

A: An outpatient coverage provision details the extent to which a health insurance policy covers medical services that do not require hospital admission, such as day surgeries, diagnostic tests, and other procedures. Policies with comprehensive outpatient coverage can significantly reduce the policyholder's financial burden for these services, ensuring broader access to necessary medical care without the need for overnight hospital stays. Reviewing outpatient coverage is crucial for individuals who anticipate needing these types of medical services.

Q: What considerations come into play with a policy's drug formulary and prescription drug coverage?

A: To find out which prescription drugs are covered by your health insurance, look at your policy's drug formulary. Policyholders should consider the comprehensiveness of the formulary, copayments, or coinsurance for medications and any restrictions on drug coverage, such as prior authorization requirements. Understanding the policy's prescription drug coverage is essential for managing medication costs, especially for those with chronic conditions requiring ongoing pharmaceutical therapy.

Q: How do riders for alternative medicine coverage in health insurance policies address the growing interest in holistic care?

A: Riders for alternative medicine coverage expand health insurance benefits to include services like acupuncture, chiropractic care, and herbal treatments, catering to the growing interest in holistic and non-traditional medical care. These riders offer policyholders the flexibility

Q: What factors are considered during the life insurance underwriting process?

A: Insurers consider factors such as age, health history, lifestyle choices (e.g., smoking, alcohol use), occupation, and family medical history. These help assess the risk level of insuring an individual and determining the policy's terms and premiums.

Q: How does medical underwriting in health insurance differ post-Affordable Care Act (ACA)?

A: Post-ACA, medical underwriting for health insurance largely ceased for individual and small group markets, when it comes to insurance, pre-existing conditions are no longer grounds for price increases or denial of coverage. However, factors like age and smoking status may still influence premiums within set limits.

Q: Why might an insurance application undergo a manual underwriting process?

A: An application may require manual underwriting if it presents unique risks not easily assessed by automated systems, such as unusual medical conditions, high-risk occupations, or complex financial situations. Manual underwriting allows for a more nuanced evaluation.

Q: What role does a paramedical exam play in the insurance underwriting process?

A: A paramedical exam, often part of the underwriting process for life and health insurance, includes a health questionnaire, measurements of vital signs, and sometimes blood and urine tests. It provides insurers with a current snapshot of the applicant's health to accurately assess risk.

Q: Can an insurance applicant be denied coverage based on the underwriting process?

A: Yes, applicants can be denied coverage if the underwriting process deems them too high a risk based on their health, lifestyle, or financial background. Insurers must balance risk management with the provision of coverage, sometimes leading to denials.

Q: What is included in the policy issuance package sent to new policyholders?

A: The policy issuance package typically includes the insurance policy document detailing coverage terms, conditions, and exclusions, a summary of benefits, identification cards (for health insurance), and information on how to access policy management tools or contact customer service.

Q: How does a policyholder change their beneficiary designation?

A: Policyholders can change their beneficiary designation by submitting a written request on a form provided by the insurer. It's essential to review and update beneficiary designations periodically or after significant life events.

Q: What happens if a policyholder misses a premium payment?

A: If a premium payment is missed, the policyholder typically enters a grace period during which coverage continues. They can still make the payment without losing coverage. If the premium remains unpaid past the grace period, the policy may lapse.

Q: Can a lapsed policy be reinstated, and what are the requirements?

A: Many insurers allow for policy reinstatement within a specific timeframe after lapse, subject to requirements such as evidence of insurability, payment of past due premiums, and potentially additional fees. Reinstatement helps policyholders regain coverage without starting a new policy.

Q: What administrative roles do agents and brokers play after policy issuance?

A: Agents and brokers provide ongoing service by assisting with policy changes, answering questions, facilitating claims, and advising on additional coverage needs. They act as intermediaries between the insurer and the policyholder to make sure smooth administration of the policy.

Q: How do insurers notify policyholders of changes to their policies or premiums?

A: Insurers are required to notify policyholders in writing of any changes to their policies or premiums, typically with advance notice. This ensures transparency and allows policyholders time to make informed decisions about their coverage.

Q: What is the importance of the policy summary in policy administration?

A: The policy summary provides an overview of the key features, benefits, exclusions, and terms of the insurance policy. It serves as a quick reference for policyholders to understand their coverage and is crucial for effective policy administration.

Q: How does electronic policy delivery benefit policyholders and insurers?

A: Electronic policy delivery offers faster access to policy documents, reduces paper waste, and lowers administrative costs. It provides a convenient way for policyholders to manage their coverage digitally and enhances insurers' policy administration efficiency.

Q: What mechanisms are in place for policyholders to dispute or appeal a decision made by their insurer?

A: Insurers provide a formal appeals process for policyholders to dispute denied claims or coverage decisions. This process typically involves submitting a written appeal with supporting documentation, after which the insurer reviews and makes a determination. Policyholders have the right to escalate their appeal if necessary, including seeking external review in some cases, to ensure a fair resolution.

Q: How do annual policy reviews benefit policyholders?

A: Annual policy reviews offer policyholders an opportunity to assess their current coverage in light of any changes in their circumstances, financial goals, or insurance needs. This proactive approach ensures that their coverage remains aligned with their objectives, allowing adjustments such as increasing coverage, adding riders, or identifying potential cost savings.

Q: Describe the process for adding a rider to an existing health insurance policy.

A: To add a rider to an existing health insurance policy, the policyholder typically needs to request the addition from the insurer, who will then assess the request based on current health status, potential underwriting requirements, and additional premium costs. Approval of the rider will result in an amendment to the policy, officially incorporating the extra coverage.

Q: What is the role of underwriting in policy renewals, particularly for health insurance?

A: For health insurance, the role of underwriting in policy renewals has diminished significantly in many regions, especially in markets affected by regulations such as the ACA, which prohibit insurers from denying coverage based on health status at renewal. However, underwriting may still adjust premiums based on broader risk pools and cost trends rather than individual health changes.

Q: How can policyholders manage the impact of rising premiums in health insurance?

A: Policyholders can manage the impact of rising premiums by reviewing their coverage annually to ensure it still meets their needs, considering higher deductible plans for lower premiums, utilizing health savings accounts (HSAs) for tax advantages, and exploring all available policy options during open enrollment periods to find the most cost-effective coverage.

Q: Explain the significance of a policy's conversion provision, particularly in term life insurance.
A: The inclusion of a conversion clause in term life insurance is of great importance as it provides the policyholder the ability to change their term policy into a permanent policy without the need for a fresh health exam. This is particularly beneficial if the policyholder's health has declined, as it ensures continued coverage and access to the benefits of permanent insurance, such as cash value accumulation, even as their insurability changes.

Q: What strategies can policyholders use to ensure their health insurance coverage keeps pace with changing healthcare laws and market trends?

A: Policyholders can stay informed about changes in healthcare laws and market trends by regularly reviewing official communications from their insurers, consulting with insurance professionals, and participating in educational sessions or webinars. Actively engaging in policy review processes and considering adjustments during open enrollment periods can ensure their coverage remains relevant and comprehensive in a rapidly evolving healthcare landscape.

Q: How do insurers address privacy and data protection concerns in policy issuance and administration?

A: Insurers address privacy and data protection concerns by implementing robust security measures compliant with relevant regulations, such as HIPAA in the U.S., to safeguard personal and medical information. They also ensure transparency in their data usage policies, provide training to staff on privacy practices, and regularly audit their systems for vulnerabilities to protect policyholder information throughout the policy lifecycle.

Q: In what situations might a policyholder consider purchasing a supplemental health insurance policy?

A: A policyholder might consider purchasing a supplemental health insurance policy to cover gaps in their primary health insurance coverage, such as high deductibles, co-payments, or services not fully covered (e.g., dental, vision, or hearing services). Supplemental policies can also provide additional financial protection against specific illnesses or accidents.

Q: How does a policy exclusion for dangerous sports or activities affect an individual's coverage?

A: A policy exclusion for dangerous sports or activities means that any injuries or health issues resulting from participation in such activities will not be covered. Individuals engaged in high-risk hobbies may need to seek additional or specialized insurance coverage to ensure they are protected against potential medical costs associated with these activities.

Q: What considerations should businesses make when choosing group health insurance policies for their employees?

A: Businesses should consider the diversity of their employees' healthcare needs, budget constraints, and the competitive landscape of employee benefits. Choosing a group health insurance policy that offers a balance of comprehensive coverage, affordability, and flexibility can help attract and retain talent while ensuring employees have access to necessary healthcare services.

Q: How do changes in a policyholder's life stage or family status impact the need for policy adjustments or reviews?

A: Changes in a policyholder's life stage or family status, such as marriage, childbirth, divorce, or retirement, can significantly impact their insurance needs and financial priorities. These life events may necessitate policy adjustments to ensure adequate coverage is in place to meet new responsibilities or to align with updated financial planning goals.

PRACTICE TEST

TEST PART 1

1. Which life insurance policy type offers flexibility in premium payments and death benefits?
A) Whole Life Insurance
B) Term Life Insurance
C) Universal Life Insurance
D) Variable Life Insurance

2. What rider provides a death benefit in addition to the base policy if the insured dies due to an accident?
A) Accelerated Death Benefit Rider
B) Guaranteed Insurability Rider
C) Accidental Death Benefit Rider
D) Waiver of Premium Rider

3. Which feature allows a term life insurance policyholder to convert their policy to a permanent one without additional evidence of insurability?
A) Conversion Option
B) Renewability Feature
C) Guaranteed Insurability Option
D) Accelerated Death Benefit Option

4. What does the incontestability clause in a life insurance policy state?
A) The insurer cannot contest the policy after it has been in force for two years, except for non-payment of premiums.
B) The policy will automatically renew without a medical exam.
C) Premiums can be adjusted based on the insured's health changes.
D) The insurer can contest the policy at any time for any reason.

5. In life insurance, what does a "Return of Premium" rider entail?
A) The insured can borrow against the policy's cash value.
B) Premiums are waived if the insured becomes disabled.
C) The policy accumulates cash value at a fixed interest rate.
D) Premiums paid are returned if the insured outlives the term of the policy.

6. How are life insurance proceeds typically taxed to the beneficiary?
A) As taxable income
B) As capital gains
C) Not taxed
D) As estate tax

7. Which type of policy is designed to provide coverage for a specific period and then expire without a cash value component?
A) Whole Life Insurance
B) Term Life Insurance
C) Universal Life Insurance
D) Variable Universal Life Insurance

8. What is the primary purpose of a long-term care rider attached to a life insurance policy?
A) To increase the policy's cash value
B) To provide coverage for the cost of long-term care services
C) To extend the term of the policy
D) To cover the cost of accidental death

9. What happens if a life insurance policy lapses due to non-payment of premiums?
A) The policy can be reinstated at any time without conditions.
B) The insurer must provide a full refund of all premiums paid.
C) Coverage ends, but the policy may be reinstated within a certain period under certain conditions.
D) The beneficiary receives a partial death benefit.

10. Which policy feature allows for an increase in death benefits based on inflation or other factors without additional medical underwriting?
A) Cash Value Option
B) Cost of Living Adjustment Rider
C) Guaranteed Renewability
D) Premium Adjustment Option

11. What is the tax implication for the cash value growth within a whole life insurance policy?
A) Taxed annually as income
B) Taxed only upon withdrawal
C) Tax-free
D) Subject to capital gains tax

12. Which rider would ensure that premiums are waived if the policyholder becomes disabled?
A) Accidental Death Rider
B) Waiver of Premium Rider
C) Guaranteed Insurability Rider
D) Term Conversion Rider

13. For a universal life insurance policy, what does the option to adjust the premium payments provide to the policyholder?
A) The ability to invest in equity markets directly
B) Flexibility in payment amounts and timing
C) A fixed interest rate on the cash value
D) Automatic coverage extension

14. In the context of life insurance, what does the term "rider" refer to?
A) A minor beneficiary
B) A temporary insurance certificate
C) An amendment or addition to a policy that modifies the coverage or terms
D) The policyholder's legal representative

15. What is the primary reason to include an accelerated death benefit rider in a life insurance policy?
A) To cover funeral expenses
B) To provide funds if the insured is diagnosed with a terminal illness
C) To increase the policy's cash value
D) To extend the policy term without requalification

16. How do dividends from a participating whole life insurance policy typically get treated for tax purposes?
A) Taxed as ordinary income
B) Tax-free, up to a specific limit
C) Tax-deductible for the policyholder
D) Subject to capital gains tax

17. What does the automatic premium loan feature in life insurance policies prevent?
A) Policy cancellation due to non-payment of premium
B) Interest accrual on borrowed cash value
C) Unauthorized changes to the policy's beneficiaries
D) Reduction of the policy's face value

18. Which provision in life insurance allows the insurer to spread the risk by requiring a medical exam only if the death benefit exceeds a certain amount?
A) Insurability Testing Provision
B) Conditional Receipt Provision
C) Medical Underwriting Provision
D) Evidence of Insurability Provision

19. What determines the premium rates for a term life insurance policy?
A) The policyholder's credit score
B) Market interest rates
C) The insured's age, health, and life expectancy at issuance
D) The number of beneficiaries named in the policy

Correct Answers and Reasons TEST PART 1

1. **Correct Answer: C) Universal Life Insurance**
    Reason: Because universal life insurance has adjustable death benefits and variable premiums, policyholders may modify their coverage as their financial circumstances change.
2. **Correct Answer: C) Accidental Death Benefit Rider**
    Reason: This rider enhances the protection afforded by the policy by adding a death benefit to the basic policy amount in the event that the insured's death is caused by an accident.
3. **Correct Answer: A) Conversion Option**
    Reason: The conversion option allows a term life policyholder to convert their policy into a permanent one without proving insurability again, providing a valuable safeguard against losing coverage.
4. **Correct Answer: A) The insurer cannot contest the policy after it has been in force for two years, except for non-payment of premiums.**
    Reason: The incontestability clause protects the policyholder from the insurer contesting the validity of the policy after a certain period, ensuring stability and peace of mind.
5. **Correct Answer: D) Premiums paid are returned if the insured outlives the term of the policy.**
    Reason: A Return of Premium rider guarantees that the insured will get their premiums returned if they live longer than the policy's term, providing both safety and savings.
6. **Correct Answer: C) Not taxed**
    Reason: Life insurance proceeds are typically received tax-free by the beneficiary, providing full financial benefits without the burden of income tax.
7. **Correct Answer: B) Term Life Insurance**
    Reason: It is designed to offer protection for a specific period, after which the policy expires without accruing any cash value.
8. **Correct Answer: B) To provide coverage for the cost of long-term care services**
    Reason: nursing home care, assisted living, and home health care are all examples of long-term care services that may be covered by an additional life insurance policy called a long-term care rider. This rider assists policyholders in managing the exorbitant expenses associated with such treatment, which are often excluded from conventional health insurance plans.
9. **Correct Answer: C) Coverage ends, but the policy may be reinstated within a certain period under certain conditions.**
    Reason: If a life insurance policy lapses due to non-payment of premiums, the coverage ceases, but most insurers offer a reinstatement period during which the policyholder can reinstate the policy by meeting specific conditions, such as paying back premiums and possibly undergoing a new health assessment. This provision helps policyholders recover their coverage even after a temporary financial setback.
10. **Correct Answer: B) Cost of Living Adjustment Rider**
    Reason: The Cost of Living Adjustment (COLA) Rider adjusts the death benefit to account for inflation or other cost-of-living increases, ensuring the policy's value remains relevant over time without the need for further medical underwriting.
11. **Correct Answer: C) Tax-free**
    Reason: The cash value increase inside a whole life insurance policy is tax-deferred, indicating that it is not subject to taxation while it grows. Taxes may be due upon withdrawal, but the growth itself accumulates tax-free.
12. **Correct Answer: B) Waiver of Premium Rider**
    Reason: The Waiver of Premium Rider ensures that the policy remains in effect without adding to the policyholder's financial burden while they are disabled by waiving the premium payments for the policy.
13. **Correct Answer: B) Flexibility in payment amounts and timing**
    Reason: Universal life insurance plans give policyholders the option to modify the time and quantity of premium payments to accommodate their financial circumstances, as long as the policy has enough cash value to meet the expenses.
14. **Correct Answer: C) An amendment or addition to a policy that modifies the coverage or terms**
    Reason: A rider is an additional provision added to an insurance policy that modifies its terms or coverage, offering policyholders customized protection to meet specific needs.

15. **Correct Answer: B) To provide funds if the insured is diagnosed with a terminal illness**

Reason: The policyholder may get a part of the death benefit early if they get a terminal disease diagnosis with the expedited death benefit rider. This offers much-needed financial assistance at a crucial period.

16. **Correct Answer: B) Tax-free, up to a specific limit**

Reason: Dividends received from a participating whole life insurance policy are regarded as a reimbursement of surplus premiums and are hence exempt from taxation, as long as they do not exceed the whole amount of premiums paid. They are not taxed as ordinary income unless the dividends exceed the total premiums paid.

17. **Correct Answer: A) Policy cancellation due to non-payment of premium**

Reason: The automatic premium loan feature allows the insurer to automatically take a loan against the policy's cash value to pay any due premiums, preventing the policy from lapsing due to non-payment.

18. **Correct Answer: D) Evidence of Insurability Provision**

Reason: The Evidence of Insurability Provision enables the insurer to require a medical exam or other proof of insurability if the requested death benefit exceeds a specified amount, helping the insurer manage risk more effectively.

19. **Correct Answer: C) The insured's age, health, and life expectancy at issuance**

Reason: Premium rates for term life insurance are primarily determined by factors that assess the risk of insuring the individual, such as the insured's age, health status, and life expectancy at the time the policy is issued. These factors help the insurer calculate the likelihood of paying out the death benefit during the policy's term.

TEST PART 2

1. What is a characteristic feature of a Preferred Provider Organization (PPO) health plan?
A) Requires referrals for specialists.
B) Offers a high deductible option only.
C) Provides flexibility in choosing healthcare providers.
D) Limits coverage to in-network providers exclusively.

2. How does a Health Maintenance Organization (HMO) plan typically manage care?
A) By allowing members to seek care outside the network at no additional cost.
B) Through a designated primary care physician who coordinates all care.
C) By offering nationwide coverage without restrictions.
D) Through a high deductible to encourage savings.

3. Which rider in a health insurance policy typically covers care in a nursing home or assisted living facility?
A) Accidental Death Rider
B) Long-Term Care Rider
C) Critical Illness Rider
D) Waiver of Premium Rider

4. What does the out-of-pocket maximum in a health insurance policy signify?
A) The minimum amount a policyholder must spend on healthcare services annually.
B) The total deductible amount for the policy term.
C) The maximum amount a policyholder will pay for covered services in a plan year.
D) The premium amount paid monthly by the policyholder.

5. Which provision allows a policyholder to remain insured without paying premiums if they become disabled?
A) Coordination of Benefits
B) Waiver of Premium for Disability
C) Guaranteed Renewal
D) Pre-existing Condition Exclusion

6. In health insurance, what is the purpose of an annual deductible?
A) The amount the insurance company pays before the policyholder pays anything.
B) The fixed fee for accessing healthcare services.
C) The amount a policyholder must pay out-of-pocket before the insurer pays for covered services.
D) The limit on the amount the policyholder can spend on healthcare in a year.

7. Which health policy provision typically excludes coverage for injuries sustained during high-risk activities?
A) Adventure Sport Exclusion
B) Coordination of Benefits
C) Network Provider Provision
D) Preventive Care Inclusion

8. What is the primary benefit of adding a critical illness rider to a health insurance policy?
A) It decreases the overall cost of the policy.
B) It covers routine check-ups and screenings.
C) It provides a lump sum benefit upon diagnosis of certain illnesses.
D) It extends coverage to family members without additional premiums.

9. How does a Health Savings Account (HSA) complement a high-deductible health plan (HDHP)?
A) By providing funds to pay for premiums.
B) By offering a tax-free way to save and pay for medical expenses.
C) By reducing the deductible amount each year.
D) By covering all medical expenses before the deductible is met.

10. What is typically covered under the preventive care benefit of a health insurance policy?
A) Elective surgeries
B) Cosmetic procedures
C) Annual physical exams and screenings
D) Expenses exceeding the out-of-pocket maximum

11. Which health insurance model requires policyholders to receive care from a specific network of providers to be covered?
A) Exclusive Provider Organization (EPO)
B) Point of Service (POS)
C) Fee-for-Service (FFS)
D) Health Reimbursement Arrangement (HRA)

12. What does a maternity coverage rider in a health insurance policy provide?
A) Coverage for prescription medications only
B) A waiver of premiums during maternity leave
C) Benefits for pregnancy, childbirth, and newborn care
D) Unlimited visits to specialists without referrals

13. Which health insurance option is specifically designed to supplement Medicare coverage?
A) Medicaid
B) Medigap
C) Employer-sponsored health insurance
D) Catastrophic health insurance

14. What is the primary function of the prescription drug coverage option in a health insurance plan?
A) To provide a discount on all over-the-counter medications
B) To limit coverage to generic drugs only
C) To cover the cost of prescribed medications, partially or in full
D) To increase the plan's deductible for medication costs

15. Which term describes the feature of an insurance policy that covers both medical and surgical expenses incurred in a hospital?
A) Hospital Indemnity Coverage
B) Comprehensive Major Medical Coverage
C) Basic Hospital Expense Coverage
D) Surgical Expense Coverage

Correct Answers and Reasons TEST PART 2

1. **Correct Answer: C) Provides flexibility in choosing healthcare providers.**
   Reason: PPO plans allow members to visit any healthcare provider, but they offer lower costs if members use providers within the plan's network, providing a balance between flexibility and cost-efficiency.

2. **Correct Answer: B) Through a designated primary care physician who coordinates all care.**
   Reason: HMO programs need members to choose a primary care physician (PCP) who serves as the primary contact for all healthcare requirements, including the provision of referrals to specialists within the network.

3. **Correct Answer: B) Long-Term Care Rider**
   Reason: The Long-Term Care Rider adds coverage for services like nursing home care or assisted living, which are not typically covered under standard health insurance policies.

4. **Correct Answer: C) The maximum amount a policyholder will pay for covered services in a plan year.**
   Reason: The out-of-pocket maximum is a limit on the total expenses that a policyholder must personally pay for covered treatments throughout the year. Once this limit is reached, the insurance company will cover 100% of the approved costs.

5. **Correct Answer: B) Waiver of Premium for Disability**
   Reason: This clause enables policyholders to maintain their health coverage without incurring premiums during times of incapacity, guaranteeing uninterrupted coverage.

6. **Correct Answer: C) The amount a policyholder must pay out-of-pocket before the insurer pays for covered services.**
   Reason: An annual deductible is a cost-sharing requirement that ensures policyholders pay a specified amount of covered healthcare costs before the insurance plan starts to pay.

7. **Correct Answer: A) Adventure Sport Exclusion**
   Reason: Many health policies include exclusions for injuries sustained from engaging in high-risk or adventure sports to mitigate the risk of costly claims from dangerous activities.

8. **Correct Answer: C) It provides a lump sum benefit upon diagnosis of certain illnesses.**
   Reason: A critical illness rider provides financial security by offering a one-time payment in the event that the insured individual is diagnosed with a certain critical disease. This payment helps to cover unforeseen medical costs or compensate for any lost income.

9. **Correct Answer: B) By offering a tax-free way to save and pay for medical expenses.**
   Reason: Individuals with high-deductible health plans (HDHPs) have an option to save for medical bills using tax-advantaged health savings accounts (HSAs). This helps with managing high deductibles and other out-of-pocket costs.

10. **Correct Answer: C) Annual physical exams and screenings**
    Reason: Preventive care benefits cover routine health checks and screenings, such as vaccinations and cancer screenings, aimed at preventing illness or detecting health issues early.

11. **Correct Answer: A) Exclusive Provider Organization (EPO)**
    Reason: EPO plans provide coverage only when members use providers within the plan's network, emphasizing managed care within a specific network of doctors and hospitals.

12. **Correct Answer: C) Benefits for pregnancy, childbirth, and newborn care**
    Reason: Maternity coverage riders enhance a health policy by covering costs related to pregnancy, childbirth, and care for newborns, addressing the specific healthcare needs associated with maternity.

13. **Correct Answer: B) Medigap**
    Reason: Medigap, or Medicare Supplement Insurance, is specifically created to fill in the gaps in coverage provided by Original Medicare. This includes expenses like copayments, coinsurance, and deductibles, providing extra financial security for those enrolled in Medicare.

14. **Correct Answer: C) To cover the cost of prescribed medications, partially or in full**
    Reason: Prescription drug coverage is a crucial part of many health plans, covering the cost of prescribed medications to reduce policyholders' out-of-pocket expenses.

15. **Correct Answer: B) Comprehensive Major Medical Coverage**
    Reason: Comprehensive Major Medical Coverage is a broad term for insurance that includes a wide range of medical expenses, including both hospital stays and surgical procedures, offering extensive protection against significant healthcare costs.

CONCLUSION

As we draw the curtains on this extensive journey through the intricacies of life and health insurance, it's clear that the landscape of insurance is as diverse as it is dynamic. This book has endeavored to lay bare the multifaceted world of insurance policies, the myriad of provisions, riders, options, and exclusions that tailor these policies to individual needs, and the critical considerations surrounding retirement, taxation, and other significant aspects impacting policyholders and beneficiaries alike.

From understanding the fundamental differences between term and permanent life insurance to navigating the complex provisions that govern policy operations, we've traversed a broad spectrum of knowledge. Exploring riders and options has illuminated how flexibility and customization in insurance can serve varied personal and financial situations, highlighting the importance of informed decision-making in policy selection.

The discussions on health insurance policy types have unpacked the various models of care and coverage, providing clarity on how each model fits into the broader healthcare landscape. By delving into provisions, riders, and exclusions specific to health policies, this guide has aimed to equip readers with the knowledge to discern the best coverage options for their healthcare needs, emphasizing the role of informed choice in securing optimal health benefits.

Retirement and taxation considerations have underscored the pivotal role of insurance in financial planning. By examining how life insurance integrates with retirement strategies and the tax implications of insurance policies, we've bridged the gap between insurance and broader financial wellness, underscoring the strategic importance of insurance in achieving long-term financial security.

Through this book, the aim has been not only to prepare readers for the Life & Health Insurance Exam but also to instill a deep understanding of the insurance sector's role in providing security and peace of mind. It is hoped that this knowledge empowers not just aspiring insurance professionals but anyone looking to navigate the complexities of insurance with confidence and acumen.

In conclusion, the journey through the world of life and health insurance is ongoing and ever-evolving. As laws change, new products emerge, and individual needs shift, the importance of staying informed and adaptable cannot be overstated. This book has sought to lay a foundation of understanding that will support readers in adapting to changes and making decisions that align with their goals and needs. Whether you are preparing for a professional exam or seeking to deepen your understanding of insurance for personal reasons, remember that the essence of insurance is protection and provision for the future. Armed with knowledge, you are well-positioned to make choices that ensure peace of mind for yourself and those you care for today and tomorrow.

EXTRA STUDY AIDS - DOWNLOAD

Dear esteemed reader, your decision to explore this book marks the beginning of an enriching path, and we are honored to walk alongside you.

Your insights are a treasure!

The experiences and reflections you gather from this book are crucial to us. We warmly invite you to share your impressions on Amazon. Whether you found a specific segment particularly meaningful, a piece of advice enlightening, or if the overall exploration of the topics has deepened your knowledge, your feedback is invaluable. By sharing your thoughts, you not only aid fellow readers in their quest for knowledge but also motivate us, the authors, to further refine and enrich our content.

A special EXTRA CONTENT PACKAGE is here for you!

As a token of our appreciation, we've prepared an exclusive set of resources tailored just for you:

- **INCLUDES AUDIOBOOK** for on-the-go learning.

- **DIGITAL COPY OF THIS BOOK** to have with you at all times for revision whenever and wherever you want.

- **XL PACK**: access the **"Property & Casualty Insurance Test Prep" in digital format** at no additional cost.

- **"GUIDE TO INSURANCE TERMS" flashcards (over 1000!)** in PDF format ready to print and in .APKG format for Anki app, for a dynamic and interactive learning experience. Elevate your study sessions by utilizing these flashcards to effortlessly recall key terms and concepts. Available for download on Anki APP, AnkiDroid, or through our website—no registration or payment required. Import the gift files and study at your leisure, tracking your progress as you go

- **Direct contact** for assistance or clarifications, ensuring continuous support in your preparation.

✦ No strings attached, just continuous learning and empowerment ✦

Find below an exclusive QR CODE, your gateway to the extra content awaiting your discovery. We promise a seamless process—no subscriptions, no personal details needed. Just our honest contribution to your educational journey.

If you encounter any issues accessing the materials, please reach out to us at **studyaiddesk@gmail.com.**

Our commitment is to make your learning experience exceptionally rewarding

With infinite gratitude,
Bennett Lane
Thank you!

Made in the USA
Las Vegas, NV
20 August 2024

94182391R00050